CREATION AND LAST THINGS

CREATION AND LAST THINGS

At the Intersection of Theology and Science

Gregory S. Cootsona

Foundations of Christian Faith
Published by Geneva Press in Conjunction with
the Office of Theology and Worship, Presbyterian Church (U.S.A.)

© 2002 Gregory S. Cootsona

Scripture quotations from the New Revised Standard Version of the Bible are copyright © 1989 by the Division of Christian Education of the National Council of the Churches of Christ in the U.S.A., and are used by permission.

Book design by Sharon Adams
Cover design by Night & Day Design

First edition
Published by Geneva Press
Louisville, Kentucky

This book is printed on acid-free paper that meets the American National Standards Institute Z39.48 standard. ∞

PRINTED IN THE UNITED STATES OF AMERICA

04 05 06 07 08 09 10 11 — 10 9 8 7 6 5 4 3

Library of Congress Cataloging-in-Publication Data

Cootsona, Gregory S.
    Creation and last things / Gregory S. Cootsona.— 1st ed.
        p. cm. — (Foundations of Christian faith)
    Includes bibliographical references.
    ISBN 0-664-50160-5 (pbk.)
    1. Creation. 2. Eschatology. I. Title. II. Series.

BT695 .C664 2002
231.7'65—dc21

2001040970

Contents

Series Foreword

*T*he books in the Foundations of Christian Faith series explore central elements of Christian belief. These books are intended for persons on the edge of faith as well as for those with strong Christian commitment. The writers are women and men of vital faith and keen intellect who know what it means to be an everyday Christian.

Each of the twelve books in the series focuses on a theme central to the Christian faith. The authors hope to encourage you as you grapple with the big, important issues that accompany our faith in God. Thus, Foundations of Christian Faith includes volumes on the Trinity, what it means to be human, worship and sacraments, Jesus Christ, the Bible, the Holy Spirit, the church, life as a Christian, political and social engagement, religious pluralism, creation and new creation, and dealing with suffering.

You may read one or two of the books that deal with issues you find particularly interesting, or you may wish to read them all in order to gain a deeper understanding of your faith. You may read the books by yourself or together with others. In any event, I trust that you will find a fuller awareness of the living God who is made known in Jesus Christ through the present power of the Holy Spirit. Christian faith is not about the mastery of ideas. It is about encountering the living God. It is my confident hope that this series of books will lead you more deeply into that encounter.

Charles Wiley
Office of Theology and Worship
Presbyterian Church (U.S.A.)

I

Getting Started

The last thing one discovers in composing a work is what to put first.

Blaise Pascal

*M*ost people do not bother with introductions, which is too bad. There authors drop their guard and give readers an easy entry into their work. There authors lay out what is really important to them. This introduction is no different. In it, I describe the topics this book will cover, why they are important to me, and finally how to use this book in an adult education class.

Deep down, we search for a reason to live. We hunger for truth and meaning in our lives. God's drama of interacting with us and our world, described through the doctrines of creation and last things (or "eschatology"), fulfill our deepest human need for a reason to live. God's creation reminds us that we are made for good. Providence describes God's continual interacting with us and our world despite the presence of evil. The ending of the world and its fulfillment in the new creation show that God is not finished with us yet.

As a member of the Foundations of Christian Faith team, I have the particular task of unfolding the doctrines of creation and eschatology in light of contemporary science. My goal is to present "mere Christianity" (the term C. S. Lewis made famous for remaining faithful to the broad consensus of the Christian tradition), while speaking meaningfully to a contemporary, scientifically minded age. As Karl Barth—surely the greatest theologian of the twentieth century—once symbolized the Christian's responsibility: we are to live with the Bible in one hand and the newspaper in the other. (By the way, except where noted I quote from the New Revised Standard Version.) Nevertheless, I am a pastor and theologian, not a scientist. And so, to use Isaac Newton's phrase, in order to see farther I have learned to "stand on the shoulders of giants." After having a dialogue with scientists for their insights, I have discerned the consensus of science at this point in its development. So, as you will see in chapters three and four, despite some engagement in the debate over the scientific and philosophical integrity of neo-Darwinianism, I am convinced that most scientists and scientifically minded theologians believe the theory stands intact. Straining out the materialistic and atheistic elements of much contemporary neo-Darwinism, I build my theological conclusions accordingly.

How do I recommend you use this book? Certainly one could read it simply for individual learning. I hope—pray, really—that it will spark both your mind and spirit and bring you to a deeper understanding of our good Creator. If I have done that in any measure, I have accomplished much and repaid a debt to those like Blaise Pascal, C. S. Lewis, Anne Lamott, and John Polkinghorne, whose writings have inspired me and led me to new intellectual and spiritual vistas. In addition, you could also easily use this book to teach a five-week adult education course. (Not surprisingly, that is the length of the classes I teach at the Fifth Avenue Presbyterian Church's Center for Christian Studies.) After a brief introduction by the teacher, the students could read one of the following four chapters before the subsequent weeks. A few basic questions could be used for each chapter: What did you learn in this chapter about the doctrine of creation (or the fall or providence or eschatology)? Where do you agree or disagree? What changes would you like to make to your life in light of this doctrine? I have also found it helpful for students to bring articles related to the science of each topic or to discuss more explicitly the biblical texts in each chapter.

This book fits best in a class specifically on creation and eschatology, but could also support a class on either. To use it as part of a general course on Christian doctrine, I would fill in with other texts from the series. The three most directly related are Leanne Van Dyk's forthcoming *Believing in Jesus Christ,* Philip W. Butin's *The*

Trinity, and Kathryn J. Cameron's forthcoming *Why Have You Forsaken Me?*

As I have studied the relationship of our Creator and the world—especially God's grace poured out in creation—I have learned again to count my blessings. I have found that we can either take the world for granted and believe that we deserve everything we receive. Or we discover that life is a miraculous gift, and there discover happiness, contentment, and peace. The second option is by far the better one. So I would like to express my great pleasure in meeting twice a year with the other Foundations authors. Ron Byars, Luther Ivory, and Leanne Van Dyk offered particularly helpful advice. Charles Wiley has coached us well as general editor and has often gone the extra mile to make our meetings enjoyable and overflowing with good food. He also suggested some substantial improvements to my manuscript in the final round of editing. Jean Umland provided some thoughtful improvements to chapter three. And, as much as I try not to have my family burdened by my writing, I am thankful for my wife, Laura, and for my children, Mel and Lizzie, who continue (in different ways) to show excitement for this book. Finally, as the millennium begins in earnest, representing an almost unimaginable step for our civilization and certainly a time of profound challenges, I am reminded to thank God the Creator, who has been lovingly interacting with this world for billions and billions of years.

Making Something out of Nothing: The Good Creation

You are worthy, our Lord and God,
  to receive glory and honor and power,
for you created all things,
  and by your will they existed and were created.
                                                    Revelation 4:11

*I want to know how God created this world. I am not inter-
ested in this or that phenomenon, in the spectrum of this
or that element. I want to know His thoughts, the rest are
details.*
                                                    Albert Einstein

*God saw everything that he had made, and indeed, it was
very good.*
                                                    Genesis 1:31a

God designed creation, and it takes our breaths away.
The glow of a full moon, the splendor of a smile, the ele-
gant beauty of nature's laws can astound us in their witness to God's master artistry in creation. They are signs
that we are always in the presence of the divine. The most
natural response is to praise the Creator. The doctrine of
creation is about the goodness of the God of life—the God
who brings things that did not exist into existence with
one simple word. It is about the God who continues to create a "new thing" throughout cosmic and human history.
It even points to the God who will fulfill creation at the
end of time.

Poetry and music express—with a greater accuracy than philosophical or scientific language—the wonder and glory of creation. The hymn of ancient Israel says it so well:

> The heavens are telling the glory of God;
>   and the firmament proclaims his handiwork.
> Day to day pours forth speech
>   And night to night declares knowledge.

(Ps. 19:1–2)

William Shakespeare lived at least two millennia later than the psalmist. Nevertheless, during the great flowering of modern science in the seventeenth century, Shakespeare found similar insight from the Book of Nature:

> And this our life, exempt from public haunt,
> Finds tongues in trees, books in the running brooks,
> Sermons in stones, and good in every thing.[1]

Finally, Gerard Manley Hopkins, the late-nineteenth-century Jesuit, produced poetry far ahead of his Victorian age. In "God's Grandeur," he expressed the surprise and power of God's glory in creation even in spite of the havoc wrought upon the world by our actions:

> The world is charged with the grandeur of God.
>   It will flame out, like shining from shook foil;
>   It gathers to a greatness, like the ooze of oil
> Crushed. Why do men then now not reck his rod?
> Generations have trod, have trod, have trod;
>   And all is seared with trade; bleared, smeared with toil;
>   And wears man's smudge and shares man's smell: the soil
> Is bare now, nor can foot feel, being shod.
>
> And for all this, nature is never spent;
>   There lives the dearest freshness deep down things;
> And though the last lights off the black West went
>   Oh, morning, at the brown brink eastward, springs—
> Because the Holy Ghost over the bent
>   World broods with warm breast and with ah! bright wings.

I write now as a Christian convinced by these truths. But this has not always been the case. I grew up in the beautiful, self-sufficient

Silicon Valley that was secular in the truest sense of the word: God simply did not play a part in our life. When we factored in the various components of our existence, there was no God, no church. The wider culture of Menlo Park, California, mirrored this casual secularity. I can certainly believe what I once heard reported: less than 10 percent of the culture of the San Francisco Peninsula can be found in church on any given Sunday. Nature in this world is certainly an object of great beauty, but is not filled with God's presence.

In college, one of the forces that drove me first to consider the world's religions, and ultimately the Christian faith, was the lack of meaning inherent in a godless world. It took some hard-fought reflection, but I learned this: joy and fulfillment come from knowing the One who made us and what our purpose is on earth. A Stradivarius works perfectly as a violin, but does not help when the floors need sweeping. Not to know the design yields frustration and futility. Living with purpose brings fulfillment. God's design for us provides the right "usage" for human life.

Mark Twain once quipped, "There are two types of people—those who divide people into two types and everyone else." With Twain in mind, I am still willing to say that there are two basic approaches to our existence: *life either bursts with meaning or is meaningless.*

And yet, on certain days which of us does not resonate with certain scientists who, having cut themselves off from the Designer, find an ultimately purposeless creation? Harvard astronomer Margaret Geller believes that it is pointless to mention purpose: "[W]hy should [the universe] have a point? What point? It's just a physical system, what point is there?"[2]

Certainly, not all scientists express similar nihilism about creation. I remember a graduate seminar on genetics and ethics with David Cole, a biochemist at the University of California at Berkeley. He showed us pictures of polymers and exclaimed—"Aren't these beautiful! Look at the wonder of God's creation!" I had never thought of polymers that way. (Actually, I had never looked at them that closely.) Like David Cole, many scientists, in discovering God's design, find ample reason to praise the Designer. In fact, I will demonstrate how science and theology in the past century have pointed toward an amazing convergence.

While working with the critical issues of this book, I have kept three sets of questions in mind:

- What is the relationship between the creation in the beginning and the new creation at the end of time? Put another way, what is the relation between the doctrine of creation and the promise of God to make "all things new"?
- What does God's creation of the world mean in light of contemporary science?
- How does the doctrine of creation inform the everyday life of Christians? Does it affect our sense of purpose and meaning? How do we grow in faith, hope, and love in light of these doctrines? How do we develop our spirituality in light of creation?

God has brought this world into existence. Both the act of doing so and the product are creation. Like a writer, God invented and created the world and, in doing so, stepped back to let the characters "speak for themselves." The created order remains different from God. On the other hand, the work bears the imprint of its Artist. Two analogies come to mind: writing a play and improvising with a jazz combo. I will save how God and Miles Davis can be compared for the moment and move instead to the analogy of writing. Speaking the world into existence has been used as an image for creation since the Hebrew Scriptures. As Psalm 33:9 declares, "[God] spoke, and it came to be." Words require no preexisting material and point to the sovereignty of the Writer of the drama. Thankfully, we know the ending, and it is all good. From an undergraduate education in French literature, I recall that a comedy is defined not by its use of humor (although there may be some) but by its ending. A comedy ends with resolution, with good ultimately in triumph over evil. And so in God's comedy, good wins out. In the meantime, the real joy will be discovering our part in this cosmic comedy.

The Good News of Creation
in Light of Contemporary Science

I have sat many times at the edge of Lake Tahoe under the summer sun, breathing the fresh mountain air and contemplating the beauty and austerity of its icy blue waters surrounded by gorgeously majestic peaks. There I find witnesses to God's mysterious power and deity. More than once, Paul's words from Romans 1:20 have come to me: "Ever since the creation of the world [God's] eternal power and divine nature, invisible though they are, have been understood and seen through the things he has made." Creation as a finished artistic product witnesses to the Master Artist. A stanza from the whimsical twentieth-century poet, e. e. cummings, describes the beauty and joy of creation:

> I thank You God for most this amazing day
> . . . .
> for everything which is natural which is infinite which is yes.[3]

In fact, the entire cosmos is an enormous Yes to God the Creator. From this wide-angle, cosmic perspective, the doctrine of creation affirms first of all that the universe began at an initial point at the command of God. It then says that the world—in all its magnitude and complexity—depends ultimately on God. Most of all, it proclaims that these affirmations are good news.

We often think that the "good news" begins in the opening chapters of the New Testament. There is, however, as much blessing pronounced in the first paragraphs of the Bible as anywhere else in the Scripture. Repeatedly in Genesis 1, God declares that creation "good" (vv. 4, 10, 12, 18, 25) and even "very good" (v. 31). This makes all the difference for how we understand the doctrine of creation.

When we think of the cosmic level, we do well to think beyond the tangible realm of space and time, and of the world that our senses describe. The most ancient churchwide statement of faith, the fourth-century Nicene Creed, speaks of God's creating things "seen and unseen." God creates not only the world that science discovers and measures, but the world of spiritual beings or angels. Since this book focuses on the relation of theology and science—and thus the tangible world (more or less)—I will not work extensively with the angelic (and demonic) realm of creation. That would require an altogether different, but thoroughly engaging, book. Still, the angelic realm keeps us reminded of the full depth of creation and the limits of even our greatest scientific discoveries.

Within the bounds of space and time, we will do well also to remember the scope of the cosmos. We need to think big. Let us never forget that our God is the creator of the universe, and natural science can point us to the grandeur of God's creation. Contemporary astrophysics portrays the enormous scale of the universe, which began fifteen billion years ago. This fact cures us of self-centeredness. If the age of the universe were reduced to twenty-four hours, human beings would only appear just two or three seconds before midnight.

Furthermore, Big Bang cosmology describes an "initial point of singularity" where time began, which scientists call $t = 0$. At this singularity, all laws of physics break down. The Belgian priest and mathematician George Lemaître spoke of $t = 0$ as a "day without yesterday," where space was infinitely curved and all energy and all matter was concentrated into a single quantum.[4] The Big Bang is derived from Albert Einstein's 1915 theory of general relativity, which pointed to an expanding universe. Einstein initially resisted this implication, preferring a universe that remained relatively static. So he fudged his equations with the "cosmological constant," which removed expansion in the universe, keeping it in relatively constant stasis. It took two powerful minds to persuade Einstein that an expanding universe—and therefore one with a beginning point—could be empirically and mathematically verified. Lemaître, who was fond of saying, "There is no conflict between science and religion," offered the theoretical structure for this expansion. The unparalleled master of astronomical observation, Edwin Hubble, provided the observational data. Their work (and others') eventually convinced Einstein that the universe was expanding. (Einstein later fumed: "If Hubble's expansion had been discovered at the time of the creation of the general theory of relativity, the [cosmological constant] would never have been introduced.")[5] Extrapolating backward, this expansion implied an initial singularity.

But Einstein would not be the only scientist in need of persuasion. In 1948, Cambridge professor Fred Hoyle and two colleagues, Herman Bondi and Thomas Gold, presented "steady state" cosmology. This theory stated that the universe was virtually unchanging and of infinite age. The cosmos always was, and always will be, the same. Hoyle did not like the implications of creation out of nothing for theological and philosophical reasons.

> Unlike the modern school of cosmologists, who in conformity with Judaeo-Christian theologians believe the whole universe to have been created out of nothing, my beliefs accord with those of Democritus who remarked "Nothing is created out of nothing."[6]

Hoyle argued forcefully for the steady state theory and disparagingly described its alternative as the "Big Bang."

In the 1950s and 1960s, these two theories vied for scientific approval. It was not until 1965 that Robert Wilson and Arno Penzias at the Bell Laboratories detected background static radiation in the cosmos. This static was so unexpected that Wilson and Penzias believed pigeons had roosted in their huge instruments. In fact they had, but once they were removed, the background static remained as "echoes" of that initial moment of explosive creation. The COBE (Cosmic Background Explorer) satellite probed outer space in 1989 and found further confirmation of this background radiation (technically, through its Far Infrared Absolute Spectrophotometer). The COBE home page[7] puts it this way:

> The cosmic microwave background (CMB) spectrum is that of a nearly perfect blackbody with a temperature of 2.725 ± 0.002 K. This observation matches the predictions of the hot Big Bang theory extraordinarily well, and indicates that nearly all of the radiant energy of the Universe was released within the first year after the Big Bang.

In a word, Big Bang cosmology has won out.

These discoveries provide an amazing consonance with the concept of creation out of nothing by God's command. Robert

Jastrow, an astrophysicist currently at the Mount Wilson Observatory and a self-described agnostic, has penned these rather striking comments on the Big Bang cosmologist who looks at the first chapters of Genesis:

> A sound explanation may exist for the explosive birth of our Universe; but if it does, science cannot find out what the explanation is. The scientist's pursuit of the past ends in the moment of creation.
>
> This is an exceedingly strange development, unexpected by all but the theologians. They have always accepted the word of the Bible: In the beginning God created heaven and earth. . . . At the moment it seems as though science will never be able to raise the curtain on the mystery of creation. For the scientist who has lived by his faith in the power of reason, the story ends like a bad dream. He has scaled the mountains of ignorance; he is about to conquer the highest peak; as he pulls himself over the final rock, he is greeted by a band of theologians who have been sitting there for centuries.[8]

Theologians have long held that creation happened "at once," and can be flattered by Jastrow's conclusions, but will be wise to continue listening to scientists' developing theories about the nature of our universe.

Finally, cosmologists now assert that the push of the Big Bang is countered by the pull of gravity, so that there is a constant push-pull in the universe with neither side definitively set to win the contest. We may end in a big crunch or a slow expansion into an amorphous heat-death, but those are issues for the final chapter. For now, the importance remains that the current universe lies exquisitely balanced between these two forces.

The Gift of Time

Time—one of the most fascinating topics for human reflection—arises from God's creation. It was the brilliant fourth-century North African rhetorician and philosopher Augustine who presented the question,

What, then, is time? There can be no quick and easy answer to that question, for it is no simple matter even to understand what it is, let alone find words to explain it. Yet, in our conversation, no word is more familiarly used or more easily recognized than "time." We certainly understand what is meant by the word both when we use it ourselves and when we hear it used by others.

What then is time? I know well enough what it is, provided that nobody asks me; but if I am asked what it is and try to explain, I am baffled.[9]

And so time is a puzzle, but also a gift. Without creation—and scientists would remind us that without matter—there is no time. God continues to relate to creation as the eternal God, as the One who is not limited by time, but encompasses time. To grasp this relationship with the temporal world, we have to look at God's entering human history in Jesus Christ. There time is "baptized" so to speak—God touches time and surrounds it with eternity. Thomas Oden, a theologian who has done much to demonstrate the importance of classical insights from ancient thinkers, summarizes the connection between Jesus Christ and time this way:

The decisive Christian analogy concerning time is that between the eternal indwelling in time and the incarnation. Brilliantly, the classical exegetes taught that the creation of time is analogous to the incarnation in this way: The Father inhabits time, just as the Son inhabits human flesh.[10]

In this light, God's eternity surrounds our time-bound world. *God is before all, in the present moment, and the One at the end of time.* The Bible clearly presents God's ability to act "before" all now exists. First Timothy 1:9—where one would never expect to find a metaphysical thought about time—describes God's grace as "given to us in Christ Jesus *before the ages began*" (my italics). In a similar vein, God comes "after" our current temporal sequence. God is described in Revelation 4:8 as the One "who was and is and is *to come*" (my emphasis). God's eternity therefore is not timelessness, but the fullness of time. You can imagine a piece of paper with a long, thin line written on it. In this analogy, time is the line and God is the surface on which it is written. Using the line, one can only sequentially advance to get from point A to point B. Yet using the paper, you can move between A and B without moving along the line. Or try another analogy: an author writing a play. The author can write in Act Two, then step back to Act One, then jump to Act Five, without any difficulty. She can even be writing more than one play at a time. God, whose eternity *encompasses* time, is not bound by a chronological sequence.

This understanding of time is reflected in the language of biblical Greek. Its two words for "time" create a distinction that instructs powerfully. *Chronos* is clock time, the rhythmic advance of minutes, hours, and days, which, surprisingly, I am told, has only dominated Western thought since public clocks became prominent in the late Middle Ages. "Does your watch keep good time?" That is the question of *chronos.* The other word for time, *kairos,* can be translated as "opportunity," or more literally "a decisive point in time," and in it is contained the sense of divine appointment, a "God incident." An event is *kairos* not because a watch says that it is five minutes before six on a Friday morning, but because all is in place and God is ready to speak. So God is not *confined* by the chains of time (*chronos*), but can fill any moment with divine Presence (*kairos*). We long for this fullness of time. We crave a ripple of eternity in the waters of time.

The Oxford scholar and twentieth-century Christian apologist, C. S. Lewis, offers an electrifying analogy for this longing as a sign of our eternal life. Our constant surprise at the flow of time (which scientists call "the arrow of time") means God created us not for temporality but for eternity. Lewis comments on the insight from 2 Peter 3:8 that for God, not only is a thousand years like one day (Ps. 90:4), but also "one day is like a thousand years." He reminds us that the Eternal can meet us at any moment, "but we have touched what is not in any way commensurable with lengths of time, whether long or short." Our hope then is to be removed from the sequence of time.

> For we are so little reconciled to time that we are even astonished at it. "How he's grown!" we exclaim, "How time flies!" as though the universal form of our experience were again and again a novelty. It is as strange as if a fish were repeatedly

surprised at the wetness of water. And that would be strange
indeed; unless of course the fish were destined to become, one
day, a land animal.[11]

This "fish" is meant to swim in the waters of eternity.

Secondly, the present moment is where we are offered real life,
or what philosophers might call actuality. Random email messages
rarely offer much wisdom, but one I received recently offered
some insight: "We call this moment the present because it is a gift."
The problem is that we often live in every other time *but* the present. Blaise Pascal, the brilliant seventeenth-century scientist and
theologian, has a profound meditation on this topic:

> Let each of us examine his thoughts; he will find them wholly
> concerned with the past or the future. We almost never think of
> the present, and if we do think of it, it is only to see what light
> it throws on our plans for the future. The present is never our
> end. The past and the present are our means, the future alone our
> end. *Thus we never actually live, but hope to live, and since we
> are always planning how to be happy, it is inevitable that we
> should never be so* [italics added].[12]

We live on the gossamer thread of time, but God wants to give us
the child's experience of "big, round hours" (to quote from *Bird
by Bird* by the brilliant writer Anne Lamott). God's gift of time is
here, but we would rather "hurry on to the next thing." So God's
gift of divine time is living each moment in its fullness. Of course,
we know there is the promise of something better, where there is
no death, decay, and the passing of beautiful moments that we
want to hold forever. Our hope then is for the fullness of time in
which we are given that actuality with duration, not just for the
knife-edge of time that we now experience. It is what the Bible
describes as "eternal life," which we experience now in part, but
will one day know in fullness.

Time structures everything we do in relating to God—and as we
learn to understand time as sanctified—we ourselves become holy
and increasingly see God's creation as good. This indeed is the
truth of the day of rest, the Sabbath, in which we "cease" (the literal meaning of *sabbath*) from our labors, and we return to the

goodness beneath our efforts. The Sabbath calls us not to commodify time because "time is money," but to see time as holy because all time is God's. The Sabbath rest reminds us of the essential goodness of the world, as the contemporary spiritual writer Wayne Muller reminds us.

> Our willingness to rest depends on what we believe we will find there. At rest, we come face-to-face with the essence of life. If we believe life is fundamentally good, we will seek out rest as a taste of that goodness. If we believe life is fundamentally bad or flawed, we will be reluctant to quiet ourselves, afraid of meeting the darkness that resides in things—or in ourselves.[13]

The unwillingness to practice the Sabbath is the sign of a culture that has forgotten the goodness of God and the essential benevolence of God's world.

Anne Lamott, in an unpublished address to the 1996 graduation class of the San Francisco Theological Seminary, summarizes what this means for pastors. It applies to any Christian who wants to sanctify time through slowing down by observing the Sabbath:

> I heard a farmer from the Midwest being interviewed on the Christian channel the other day, saying the reason he didn't hurry up was that he figured that when we was rushing around, he passed up more than he caught up with.
>
> Believe me, we do not need more hassled, bitter ministers. We don't want you to talk the talk, about this being the day the Lord hath made and that we should rejoice and savor its beauty and poignancy; when secretly you're tearing around like the white rabbit; we need you to walk the walk. And we need you to walk a little more slowly.

Finally, at the beginning, God creates a future for us. To create is to initiate the sequence of time we know as the past, present, and future. To understand that there is not just "now," but a time that will be, is essential to our humanity. To live as human beings means that we can envision the future, to conceive of times that will be different from what is now. We need the hope of the future, and of God's fulfilled new creation breaking into the present. Eternity is the presence of that fullness at any moment.

These past, present, and future angles of time are all reenacted and embodied in the Lord's Supper, in which Christ is there in the bread and wine. There in worship, in a way similar to the incarnation itself, the eternal can be found in the temporal. Our future home with Christ can come to the here and now at the corner of Fifth and Fifty-fifth in the wooden pews of Fifth Avenue Presbyterian. There we remember the past, Christ's death on the cross. There we celebrate the present, Christ's presence by the Holy Spirit. And there we anticipate the future—eating and drinking "until he comes" again (1 Cor. 11:26). There time becomes sanctified.

Trinitarian Creation
and the Problem of Pluralism

Creation is a team effort. And that team is the Trinity. All persons of the Trinity have it on their job description to create, but each has to create with a slightly different function. The Father initiates. The Son shapes. And the Spirit invigorates. The best way to get clear about the Christian doctrine of creation is to understand it from the perspective of the Trinity. Why? Because the Trinity itself reveals that God is a God of relationships among the three persons of the Father, the Son, and the Spirit. This love overflows in creation and calls us to enter into relationship with—to quote the jazz saxophonist John Coltrane—a Love Supreme.

The Trinity can be easily summarized: God is one in essence, yet three in the persons of the Father, the Son, and the Holy Spirit. This compact definition requires some unpacking. The Trinity is founded on two teachings of the Bible. First of all, there is only one God (the heritage of Jewish monotheism), confessed in Deuteronomy 6:4: "The Lord is our God, the Lord alone." It is stated most directly in the later chapters of Isaiah; for example, "There is no other god besides me, a righteous God and a Savior" (Isa. 45:22). Second, the Father, the Son, and the Holy Spirit are all said to be divine or to be God, as reflected in Matthew 28:19, where the disciples are commanded to baptize in "the name [in the singular, representing God's oneness or unity] of the Father and the Son and the Holy Spirit" (the three persons of the Godhead). As verses fifteen and sixteen of the Athanasian Creed put it: "So the Father is God, the Son is God, and the Holy Ghost is God. And yet they are not Three Gods, but One God." (For more elaboration, see Philip Butin's contribution to this series, *The Trinity*.)

The significance of the Trinity for the Christian life meets us at the crossroads with the doctrine of creation: God has really interacted with the created order in Jesus Christ and continues through the ongoing presence of the Spirit. Creation exists because of God's overflowing love, which first flourishes within God's own nature. Human beings are invited into a relationship with this loving Creator not only individually, but especially as a community, the church. The promise of the Trinity is that God is not far off, but holds all creation near in love.

This all sounds comforting, but how does this help me in an often chaotic and splintered life? The microwave and the contemporary sitcom remind us that life is no longer singular, unified. We are splintered into a thousand different worlds—where I "nuke" my vegetarian lasagna at 5:45, my daughter takes out a burrito to heat at 6:15, and my wife pulls out her steaming penne with meat sauce after a long workday at 9:25. No longer do we find ourselves around the common world of the dinner table. In a similar vein, no longer does the unified, confident world of the Cleavers exist. "Seinfeld"—though it too could not last forever—a TV show about "nothing"—had a vast array of single characters, seeking a way in an amoral multiverse. It represented the quintessential postmodern sitcom.

Philosophers have coined the term *postmodern* to describe the multiverse created by the variety of "languages" or perspectives by which we understand the world. This splintered existence of postmodernity, according to the theologian Stanley Grenz, destroys the concept of a singular world and thus one "worldview." It

> affirms that the world is not a given, an object "out there" that encounters us and that we can gain knowledge about. On the contrary, it affirms that through language we create our world

and that there are as many differing worlds as world-creating languages.

This plurality of worlds marks the postmodern ~~world~~ view.[14]

The "plurality of worlds" raises a particular question: How can one believe that God created *the* (one) *world?* Is there any way to sew together the varied patches of postmodern reality into a single whole? Can the triune God piece together the shards of our fragmented lives? Can God actually bring us wholeness?

In this respect, creation by God as Trinity makes a major contribution: God created the world as both multidimensional and unified. This diverse and unified God makes a diverse and unified world. To understand creation properly, one must hold together the multidimensional reality of the world as well as its unity. Eras tend to do better with the diversity or the unity. The pluralism of postmodernity underscores the multiplicity of the world. The Enlightenment, built on the strength of scientific reasoning, reigned supreme from the mid-1600s to the late eighteenth century. It held together the unity under the category of Reason. At one point during the height of the French Revolution, these disciples of the Enlightenment literally crowned an actress in Notre Dame Cathedral as the goddess of Reason. For any student of history, this action should have served as a sign of excess and a dire indication of the future. Rationalism is a stern monarch and has trouble accounting for true diversity among its subjects. Of course, contemporary pluralism has difficulty bringing the world together, and either of these emphases distorts the conjunction of multiplicity and unity that reflects the three-in-one God.

Generally, we think of God the Father as Creator. In the Hebrew Scriptures, our Old Testament, the Creator of the heavens and the earth is simply the one God. "In the beginning, God created the heavens and the earth" (Gen. 1:1 ASV). This is the only One to be worshiped, as Isaiah 45:18 declares:

> For thus says the LORD,
> who created the heavens
>   (he is God!),
> who formed the earth and made it

> (he established it;
> he did not create it a chaos,
>   he formed it to be inhabited!):
> I am the LORD, and there is no other.

But that is not the whole story: God the Father creates through the Son. The Fourth Gospel expands on these earlier texts, especially Genesis 1, using a buzzword of his day, *logos,* which implied then something like "the laws of nature" does today for many physicists. To describe the work of the Son in creation, John makes a scientific statement when he writes that the *logos* indeed mediates creation. The *logos* creates "in the beginning," a direct quotation of Genesis 1:1:

> *In the beginning* was the Word (*logos*), and the Word was with God, and the Word was God. He was in the beginning with God. All things came into being through him, and without him not one thing came into being. What has come into being in him was life, and the life was the light of all people. The light shines in the darkness, and the darkness did not overcome it. (John 1:1–5, my italics)

And so John 1 affirms that creation is *through the Son or the Logos:* "through" in v. 3 indicates that the Logos is both the agent and the pattern of creation. In other words, when we look into the eyes of Jesus Christ, we see something of the deepest structure of the universe. Our Creator God formed the universe through grace and truth, embodied in the life and ministry of Christ. This affirmation is reflected in two other New Testament texts, Colossians 1:16 and Hebrews 1:2 (italics added):

> [In the Son] all things in heaven and on earth were created, things visible and invisible, whether thrones or dominions or rulers or powers—all things have been created *through him* and *for him.*

> [B]ut in these last days he [God] has spoken to us by a Son, whom he appointed heir of all things, *through whom* he also created the worlds.

In addition to Christ's mediation of creation, the text from Colossians indicates the goal of creation: God the Father created for the

Son ("for him"). The pinnacle of creation is the incarnation: God's work as Creator finds its most intimate expression in Christ's becoming human. The world is drawn into the incarnate, risen Lord "who fills all in all" (Eph. 1:22).

What is the role of the Holy Spirit in creation? The biblical texts are fewer, and yet one encounters the question on the first pages of the Bible. Although the full doctrine of the Holy Spirit awaits New Testament revelation, God's Spirit hovers over the primordial waters in Genesis 1:2. Here God's "breath," "wind," or "spirit" reveals a characteristic of God, namely divine power. The Spirit brings life to creation. In fact, Psalm 104:29–30 makes a more direct statement of the Spirit's work in creation: "When you hide your face, they are dismayed; when you take away their breath, they die and return to their dust. When you send forth your spirit, they are created; and you renew the face of the ground." God's Spirit in the Hebrew Bible is the Lord's power in creation and ultimately in life-giving. In Genesis 2:7, God's breath makes *adam* a "living being."

Thoughtful theologians have reflected on the work of God as Trinity in creation. For example, the thirteenth-century philosophical and theological giant Thomas Aquinas ponders the question, "Is creation proper to any one divine Person?"

> For in the Creed, to the Father is attributed that "He is the Creator of all things visible and invisible"; to the Son is attributed that by Him "all things were made"; and to the Holy Ghost that He is "Lord and Life-Giver"—*[therefore] to create is not proper to any one Person, but is common to the whole Trinity. . . .* God the Father made the creature through his Word, which is His Son; and through His Love, which is the Holy Ghost [who] quickens what is created by the Father through the Son [my emphasis].[15]

Creation by the trinitarian God gets personal. The twentieth-century theologian Catherine Mowry LaCugna has revived this central aspect of the doctrine of the Trinity: "The life of God is not something that belongs to God alone. *Trinitarian life is also our life.*"[16] God's triune nature means that God our Creator is linked with the world. To use an analogy, we are like children playing in the sandbox. Our father could simply shout, "I love you!" from the kitchen window. Instead he jumps in and plays with us, creating sand castles, pushing around the toy dump truck with us. In other words, God becomes like us to love us.

And these children in the sandbox are stunningly diverse, but I believe that the world's diversity is a component of God's creativity. To change the metaphor, the Holy Spirit works—in contrast to discordant diversity—not to obliterate distinctions, but to harmonize them in a greater diverse unity. In this respect, the day of Pentecost in Acts 2 reflects the diversity in church as a microcosm of the world. These various tongues form a symphony, with its many instrumental voices and diverse notes creating melody, countermelody, and harmony. We may experience this diversity as chaotic as the tongues of Pentecost. Yet all these multifold voices blend harmoniously—and I take the metaphorical intent of this word seriously in that harmony can only exist when more than one note is played—to sing of the creative work of the one God.

Admittedly we are simply beginning musicians, most of time out of tune and cacophonous. But we are tuning our instruments for a heavenly orchestra. There the goodness of creation, in the form of universal reference to the one true, good God will be brought to its full expression only at the point of eschatological consummation, when God creates a new heaven and new earth. But that final chapter of God's creation awaits a few more chapters of this creation!

God Seen through Creation:
General Revelation

In response to this intricate theology, I can hear someone reply: "Last weekend, I spent time in the mountains, gazing across the lake, listening to the wind through the trees. In the quiet of nature, I had a direct encounter with God. I learned more about God there than I ever do in church. In the worship service, I hear *about* God. There I actually touched my Creator."

Many people, religious or not, find the palpable presence of God in creation. And here a few definitions help. In theological language, we enter the realm of *general revelation,* where God is available "generally," to all human beings. Theologians contrast it—or complement it—with *special revelation,* God's particular acts and communication with the covenant people of Israel and the church. In either general or special revelation, *God* is still the One revealing. A related area, *natural theology,* takes the data of nature and seeks to build a theological system, and I will return to it in describing the science and theology interface.

As I have already indicated, through the world we find beauty, we hear God's voice through discovery, and, as I will elaborate in the next chapter, we see God's image in one another. The natural awareness of God can lead to great wisdom, even the wisdom of Christ. John's prologue (1:9), as it introduces Jesus, says of him, "The true light, which enlightens everyone, was coming into the world."

John Calvin—and those who follow him—have contributed to a further refinement to the general revelation and its limits. In his vastly influential 1559 *Institutes of the Christian Religion,* Calvin wrote, "There is within the human mind, and indeed by natural instinct, an awareness of divinity" (1.3.1). He pointed to a sense of the numinous, powerful and brooding. "Where can I go from your spirit? Or where can I flee from your presence?" cries the psalmist in Psalm 139. It is the feeling of being out in a forest at night, knowing that no one is there, but feeling *something.* Most often, this experience disquiets us. Calvin continues,

> Though the conviction may occasionally seem to vanish for a moment, it immediately returns, and rushes in with a new impetuosity, so that any interval of relief from the gnawings of conscience is not unlike the slumber of the intoxicated or the insane, who have no quiet rest in sleep, but are continually haunted with dire horrific dreams. Even the godless themselves, therefore, are an example of the fact that some idea of God always exists in every human mind. (*Institutes* 1.3.2)

But what is the nature of this awareness of God? Calvin writes that it is "fleeting and vain" (*Institutes* 1.3.3). This is not a sturdy foundation for faith. It is the general awareness of a Supreme Being, which Paul describes in the opening chapter of Romans: "Ever since the creation of the world his eternal power and divine nature, invisible though they are, have been understood and seen through the things he has made" (1:20). Though universal and powerful, this general sense of God has a remarkable malleability. It can be the basis of nature worship, built on a sense of numinous natural world. It can be a brash, hedonistic worship of self, embodied in the basest forms of New Age spirituality. The Nazis in fact propagated an appreciation for what "God is doing through the German folk" and supported it with the powerful but vague feeling of the Transcendent working to renew the German civilization.

This vague awareness too cannot *prove* God. And that is the weakness of natural theology. Nature gives us both stunning sunsets and devastating hurricanes, fertile farmlands and windswept dust bowls, impressive mountain peaks and deadly volcanoes. Nature's supporting data present evidence of two incompatible visions: the gracious, loving God and an angry, evil deity. Pascal, who plumbed the depths of such natural proofs for God, grasped the essential weakness of this approach.

> I marvel at the boldness with which these people presume to speak of God. In addressing their argument to unbelievers, their first chapter is the proof of God from the works of nature. . . . this is giving them cause to think that the proofs of our religion are indeed feeble. . . . It is a remarkable fact that no canonical author has ever used nature to prove God.[17]

What then is the purpose of nature and this natural awareness of divinity in leading us to God? It is not a proof, but a *witness,* a support for the God revealed in Jesus Christ. We need to fill in our natural awareness of God with specificity. Only after we have heard God's voice to us in Jesus Christ, *then* we are able to proclaim with the psalmist that "The heavens are telling the glory of God" (Ps. 19:1). Scripture, as Calvin concluded, becomes the "spectacles" by which we view the world (*Institutes* 1.6.1).

Science acts in some ways as general revelation. Through general revelation, we can certainly find out truths about God, but those truths receive clarity through God's special revelation in history, especially depicted in the pages of the Bible. For example, we can find the beauty of God's design of the human body through scientific work—and thus be led to conclude that God is an incomparable Designer. We can, however, only know that God's creation is Trinitarian through special revelation.

Science and Theology: Perfect Together?

Christians are free to gaze into Galileo's telescope. We can joyfully approach scientific insights into our cosmos because knowledge about creation brings us closer to the Creator. Galileo Galilei and certainly Isaac Newton, who wrote almost as much about theology as science, would have agreed on this point. But then again so would most of the great contributors to the scientific revolution have agreed . . . like Johannes Kepler and Nicolaus Copernicus.

But the story so often heard depicts a rivalry between theology and science. One of the greatest American novelists, John Updike, has described this split with characteristic clarity though not with complete accuracy. Nonetheless, he presents a common caricature:

> Whenever theology touches science, it gets burned. In the sixteenth century astronomy, in the seventeenth microbiology, in the eighteenth geology and paleontology, in the nineteenth Darwin's biology all grotesquely extended the world-frame and sent churchmen scurrying for cover in ever smaller, more shadowy nooks, little gloomy ambiguous caves in the psyche where even now neurology is cruelly harrying them, gouging them out from the multifolded brain like wood lice from under the lumber pile.[18]

What better instance of Updike's assessment than the infamous 1633 trial of Galileo? It seems to present a clear-cut case, in which the church refused the truth as it clung to dogmas. When the eighteenth-century French *philosophes,* propagandists for the Enlightenment, argued their case for scientific reasoning and against revealed religion, they used this trial and subsequent banishment of Galileo as Exhibit A. In her brilliant book *Galileo's*

Daughter, Dava Sobel has commented, "For although science has soared beyond his quaint instruments, it is still caught in his struggle, still burdened by an impression of Galileo as a renegade who scoffed at the Bible and drew fire from a Church blind to reason."[19]

In fact, better historical analysis provides a more nuanced picture and that would unburden a popular view of Galileo's trial. The story can begin with Nicolaus Copernicus, himself no foe of the church, but of one of its "canons" or teachers. Copernicus began to present a heliocentric version of the universe in the 1530s. The previous, antithetical view, presented by Ptolemy in the second century A.D., placed the earth at the center of the universe—in accordance with Aristotle—*because the earth was the coldest and most impure place in the cosmos and farthest from the outer realms of heaven.* A geocentric view therefore had little to do with an overevaluation of the earth. The Roman Catholic Church's determination to cling to it had much to do with its dogged insistence on the truth of Aristotelian philosophy. At any rate, Copernicus's actual published theory, *De Revolutionibus,* did not appear until 1543, as Copernicus lay dying. This theory proved to be startling, but not altogether convincing. The biggest problem was that it made no improvement on understanding planetary movement.

Enter Galileo Galilei, a flamboyant and brilliant personality. As professor of mathematics in Padua, he became convinced of the truth of Copernicanism in the early 1600s. By 1616, he received a caution from Cardinal Bellarmine of the Holy Office not to treat this theory as fact, but as *hypothesis.* Why? Above all, Copernican astronomy contradicted the writings of both Aristotle and Ptolemy as well as some interpretations of Scripture. Galileo gave a blithe "okay," but continued his work. Then Maffeo Barberini, an early admirer of his work, became Pope Urban VIII in 1623. Galileo continued his work, which eventually produced the 1632 *Dialogue Concerning the Two Chief World Systems—Ptolemaic and Copernican.* It ostensibly presented both sides, but made the speaker for the geocentric view rather unsympathetic and simpleminded. He is called Simplicio, which sounds like the sixth-century Greek commentator on Aristotle, Simplicius, but also like the Italian *sempliciotto,* i.e., simpleton. Worse still, Simplicio appeared to mirror the opinions of the new pope. The next year, Galileo, almost seventy, was brought before the authorities and questioned. Despite friends near the trial and compelling testimony, he lost his case against the Inquisition. This ailing, aging man, arthritic and suffering from a double hernia, recanted his scientific conclusions under extreme pressure and fear of severe punishment. He fell under house arrest, returning eventually to his home in Arcetri near the convent of his two cloistered daughters. There he continued his scientific work until his death in 1642.

Case closed? Religion wins the battle but loses the war, right? In many ways, the standard treatment gets things right, but not without a few problems:

- *Personal:* Galileo seemed to betray a former friend, Barberini, now pope. Furthermore the pope had appeared soft on defending Catholic interests in the Thirty Years' War, largely between Catholics and Protestants. He could not deal leniently with attacks on the truth of Catholic doctrine.
- *Scientific:* As yet unexplained facts remained; Galileo could not account properly for tides, for example. He doggedly refused to follow Kepler's view (Kepler was Protestant) that they were caused by the moon, instead believing that the earth's movement was responsible.
- *Political:* The Catholic Church found itself embroiled in a battle over its truth and in a massive Counter-Reformation effort. Would it stand for the second greatest challenge to its authority after that of Calvin and Luther?
- *Scripture:* How do we interpret the biblical passages that would support either viewpoint? How, for example, could the sun have stood still at Joshua's command in Joshua 10:12–14?

The actual facts of 1633 are certainly more complex than the caricature, but infinitely less fun for those who favor tidy sound bites. The church and the scientific community—as much as those could be separated in the seventeenth century—were caught in a struggle for truth, and when Galileo was poised to win his point based on science, the church used its ecclesiastical power. And so the Catholic Church—and this goes for Christians ever since— should never have refused to look into Galileo's telescope. As the pope correctly declared in 1983, the Roman Inquisition mishandled Galileo. This fact has marred the public's perception of the relationship between science and religion. In its own day, scientific advancement after Galileo moved from Catholic Italy northward toward Protestant England, and specifically fell on the shoulders of Isaac Newton (born coincidentally in 1642, the year Galileo died).

Science and theology certainly continued their tussle in a variety of forms in the following centuries, but it never was a simple conflict. A commentator on science, Margaret Wertheim, has concluded, "The idea of a long-standing war between science and religion is a historical fiction invented in the late nineteenth century."[20] Newton, the key figure in formulating the "modern" scientific worldview, combined a rigorous faith with the most penetrating mind to come along for centuries. Admittedly, Newton strayed from orthodoxy on certain theological points—especially the Trinity—but remained committed to the Bible throughout his distinguished career. As he remarked, "No sciences are better attested than the religion of the Bible."[21] (I will discuss the case of Darwin and evolution in the next chapter.)

Still, the contemporary Nobel laureate Stephen Weinberg—like many other scientists—propagates the common notion of the incompatibility between religion and science with force: "One of the great achievements of science has been, if not to make it impossible for intelligent people to be religious, then at least to make it possible for them not to be religious. We should not retreat from this accomplishment."[22] But this conflict model oversimplifies a more varied historical interaction between these two disciplines. Consider another example, that of a nineteenth-century scientist and Christian, James Clerk Maxwell, whose theories gave inspiration to Einstein's special relativity: "Happy is the man who can recognize in the work of today a connected portion of life, and an embodiment of the work of Eternity."[23]

In this spectrum between outright oil-and-water and a chummy friendship, a number of points exist. The doyen of the study of science and theology, Ian Barbour, has set out a clear typology for four ways that religion and science have interacted.[24]

1. *Conflict*—each sees the other as an enemy and attacks its adversary. Many conservative theologians understand that science is "godless" (as some in fact is) and set their attack accordingly. On the other side, *scientism* defines all reality by what can be discovered scientifically. That approach obviously does not leave much room for faith.

2. *Independence* remains perhaps the most popular approach. Galileo is sometimes quoted in this regard: "Religion tells us how to go to heaven. Science tells us how the heavens go." (Galileo had more to say as I will note below.) The independence model has the virtue of maintaining a proper *freedom* for both science and theology. But as Philip Johnson, law professor at the University of California, Berkeley, has pointed out, "separate but equal" had disastrous effects for law in the Jim Crow South. It similarly leads to the conclusion that science deals with "the real world" and religious faith can be placed on the same level as belief in Santa Claus or unicorns—comforting, but deluded.[25]

3. *Dialogue,* where the two disciplines sit down and calmly discuss their respective insights. This is polite coffee talk—quite enjoyable, but no one is brought to changed opinions after the conversation. Many science-theology specialists find this to be the dominant, and often frustrating, pinnacle of interactions at most conferences. It ultimately splits the one world God has made into airtight microworlds.

4. *Integration* has as its goal a real learning on both sides. In this case, there is a give and take, where real transformation of thought can occur. Curiously, Galileo offers an excellent example of this approach. He understood his work as necessary for maintaining the truth of Christianity so that faith would not be wedded to bad science. For this reason, Galileo looked to God as his final arbiter after his infamous trial: "He knows that in this cause for which I suffer, though many might have spoken with more learning, none, not even the ancient Fathers, have spoken with more piety or with greater zeal for the Church than I."[26]

Throughout this book, I will seek to move toward the integration of theology and science. Nonetheless, in order for the two disciplines really to integrate, one needs to admit the similarities and differences in their approaches. Sometimes, as their respective research programs develop, dialogue may be the apex of their interaction at any moment and integration remains a goal on the horizon.

How then to move toward integration? First of all, both disciplines prize *humility*—the fact that we do not know everything. There is an incompleteness to our knowledge, but a confidence that we can learn something. Einstein definitely knew this virtue: "One thing I have learned in a long life: that all our science, measured against reality is primitive and childlike and yet it is the most precious thing we have." The Bible says it another way: "God opposes the proud, but gives grace to the humble" (Jas. 4:6). Unfortunately both Christianity and science have often proceeded without humility.

Secondly, there is a strong historical relation between the growth of science and monotheistic religion. Put simply, science has grown historically in Jewish, Christian, and Islamic countries. Why? All traditions—and I will speak primarily as a Christian—speak of God's rationality and prize the intelligibility of God's design of the universe. Copernicus stated simply, "The universe has been wrought for us by a supremely good and orderly Creator."[27] Scientific research relies on the order, coherence, and comprehensibility in nature. In fact, the development of modern science is related to the idea that nature has a pattern or "laws," which can be discerned through observation. The Nobel laureate Charles Towne, in a lecture on the relationship between the Christian faith and modern science, summarizes this connection: "For successful science of the type we know, we must have faith that the universe is governed by reliable laws and, further, that these laws can be discovered by human inquiry."[28] Conversely, to believe in the intelligibility of the universe without this basis is an amazing leap of faith.

In this respect, science and theology have much to learn from one another. Einstein provided one brilliant summary: "Science without religion is lame, religion without science is blind."[29] Pope

John Paul II formulated another: "Science can purify religion from error and superstition; religion can purify science from idolatry and false absolutes. Each can draw the other into a wider world, a world in which both can flourish."[30]

Nonetheless, there is a strong dissimilarity. Methodologically, science believes that reason is ultimate. Christianity certainly prizes reason as a gift from God, but sees its limits. Though reason can help, ultimately faith is the means for truly perceiving God. Or put another way, *God and the world are different*. God creates as an artist, but we would be silly to think the artist is the art. We may learn a great deal from the painting without seeing the painter, but never so much as when the artist speaks for herself.

Since this is true, Christians must avoid the "God of the gaps" strategy. Frequently in the past, when scientific theories lacked an explanation for a particular gap in the chain of natural phenomena, theologians and scientists inserted God. Newton, for example, could not completely account for planetary motion. There, he asserted, God must wind the watch from time to time. But as has happened with almost every gap to date, later work fills in the gaps and the need for God evaporates (as Pierre Laplace later did with Newton). The "God of the gaps" turns out to be no God at all.

The failure of the God of the gaps has great theological significance: God is not to be found at the margins of our knowledge and of life, but at the center. In fact, God should never be sought at the gaps—they only reveal human ignorance. As the brilliant nineteenth-century Harvard scientist Asa Gray put it, "I do not approve either the divinity [theology] or the science of those who are prompt to invoke the supernatural to cover our ignorance of natural causes."[31] Keeping God at the center also applies more broadly. In seeking the best way to speak of God in "a world come of age," in a culture that had largely forgotten God in its cultural and scientific pursuits, the twentieth-century German theologian and martyr Dietrich Bonhoeffer offered a profound challenge:

I've come to be doubtful of talking about human boundaries. . . .
It always seems to me that we are trying to reserve some space
for God; I should like to speak of God not on the boundaries but
at the center, not in weakness but in strength; and therefore not in
death and guilt but in man's life and goodness. . . . God is beyond
in the midst of life.[32]

Relating insights from theology and natural science (and any other
human form of knowledge) presents a delicate task. The seventeenth-
century philosopher and scientist Blaise Pascal lived at the birth of
modern science and understood the distinction between science and
faith well, and therefore could offer a profound way of relating the
two. A precocious child, Pascal made his debut in mathematics at
seventeen with his paper on conical sections and blossomed into
one of the finest scientists in the Age of Genius. He also knew life's
pain. Sickly throughout his life, he had serious bouts with illness
and at times paralysis. A Christian since childhood, he had a profound two-hour encounter with the Living God at age 31 on 23
November 1654. The experience so strongly transformed Pascal
that, for the next eight years, he carefully sewed and unsewed "the
Memorial" in the lining of his coats. It begins with these famous
lines:

FIRE

God of Abraham, God of Isaac, God of Jacob,
not of the philosophers and scholars.

Pascal knew that the profound insights of science can leave
human beings dessicated of meaning and purpose. Science, and
its servant reason, are good, but faith needs both habits or religious practices and, most of all, God's movement through the
Holy Spirit:

There are three ways to believe: reason, habit, inspiration.
Christianity, which alone has reason, does not admit as its true
children those who believe without inspiration. It is not that it
excludes reason and habit, quite the contrary, but we must open
our mind to the proofs, confirm ourselves in it through habit,

while offering ourselves through humiliations to inspiration, which alone can produce the real and salutary effect. *Lest the Cross of Christ be made of none effect.*[33]

If we are to be fruitful in bringing together science and theology, we will do well to heed Pascal's words. Though we may learn much through scientific discovery, to meet the Living God, we need the Holy Spirit.

Faith and the Meaningful Creation

As an enthusiastic young undergraduate, I will never forget sitting in the semicircular, '70s-designed, "modern" sanctuary of the First Presbyterian Church of Berkeley. There, surrounded by its purple carpet and orange pew cushions, I heard an electrifying sermon by the energetic pastor Earl Palmer on the good news of creation. His text? John 1. I listened as a relatively recent convert. Though convinced by the truth of the Christian faith, I heard then for the first time of the difference that a view of God's care for the entire creation, that God spoke the world into existence, and that we are created for a purpose and because of love. Earl contrasted this conviction with a first century filled with philosophical despair, with a heavy dose of Greek skepticism. God's good decision to create means our lives have meaning.

Today the contrast is no less marked. The conclusions represented by science and the despair of much nihilistic, postmodern philosophy do not offer a real sense of purpose or belonging. Weinberg has again stated the problem with great precision: "The more the universe seems comprehensible, the more it also seems pointless,"[34] and he can continue only by asserting that finding a unified theory could bring meaning and dignity to human existence.

Thankfully, that is one thing we do not have to believe as Christians—that the world is meaningless. We do not have to succumb to despair. Nor do we have to make meaning through our own activities. The more we read God's work—through the Book of Scripture or the Book of Nature—the more meaningful it becomes.

And that is at least part of what the Bible means by *faith*. Here I turn to John Calvin, who summarized faith as the simple trust in God's goodness extended to us in Jesus Christ. Faith grasps the essential goodness of creation. It is "a firm and certain knowledge of God's benevolence toward us, founded upon the truth of the freely given promise in Christ, both revealed to our minds and sealed in our hearts through the Holy Spirit" (*Institutes* 3.2.7). May we all have such faith.

3

Image Is Everything:
Humanity in the Image of God

So God created humankind in his image,
in the image of God he created them;
   male and female he created them.
. . . [T]hen the LORD God formed man from the dust of the
   ground,
and breathed into his nostrils the breath of life;
and the man became a living being.

Genesis 1:27; 2:7

When we consider what religion is for mankind and what
science is, it is no exaggeration to say that the future
course of history depends upon the decision of this gener-
ation as to the relations between them.

Alfred North Whitehead

*A*lexander Pope announced succinctly, "To err is human, to forgive divine." The same phrase slips easily off our lips, but it may signal a misunderstanding about our nature. God certainly forgives, but are humans fundamentally beings that err? What about the beauty and glory of humanity? Significantly, the Bible does not begin with sin. It first reminds us that to be human is to bear the glorious mark of our Creator. Genesis 1:27's compact declaration is as profound as it is brief: "So God created *adam* (Hebrew for 'human being') in his image." In this sense, Christians can agree with the slogan: "Image is everything." But we mean something much more substantial—God's image.

The Goodness of Humankind
Created in God's Image

Psalm 8 poetically depicts the glory of our human life. It uses a phrase in v. 4 (altered here for clarity), "son of *adam*"—a generic term for a human being as well as a pointer to our connection with the first human, Adam, of Genesis 1.

> [1]O LORD, our Lord,
>   how majestic is your name in all the earth!
>
> You have set your glory above the heavens.
>   [2]Out of the mouths of babes and infants
> you have founded a bulwark because of your foes,
>   to silence the enemy and the avenger.
>
> [3]When I look at your heavens, the work of your fingers,
>   the moon and the stars that you have established;
> [4]what are human beings that you are mindful of them,
>   the son of *adam* that you care for him?
>
> [5]Yet you have made them a little lower than God,
>   and crowned them with glory and honor.
> [6]You have given them dominion over the works of your hands;
>   you have put all things under their feet,
> [7]all sheep and oxen,
>   and also the beasts of the field,
> [8]the birds of the air, and the fish of the sea,
>   whatever passes along the paths of the seas.
>
> [9]O LORD, our Lord,
>   how majestic is your name in all the earth!

There is so much more to being human than erring. Above all, we are created good. We are designed to be in relationship with our Creator. Only by the abuse of freedom do we mar God's image and break our relationship with God and with creation. Abuse of freedom is, in a word, sin. But that is the topic for the next chapter. The central question for now is, What then is the image of God? The key text is Genesis 1:26–27:

26Then God said, "Let us make humankind in our image, according to our likeness; and let them have dominion over the fish of the sea, and over the birds of the air, and over the cattle, and over all the wild animals of the earth, and over every creeping thing that creeps upon the earth."

27So God created *adam* in his image,
in the image of God he created them;
male and female he created them.

Three times this passage describes human beings as being created in "the image" of God and once with a similar phrase, "according to our likeness." Theologians have considered the nature of this divine image and offered multiple answers throughout Christian history. Some have suggested that the image of God is manifested in human rationality, moral action, freedom, dominion or authority over creation, and relationality (the ability and need to relate to others). All suggestions have some merit. Relationality and its subset, dominion over creation, have the most support from the text of Genesis 1.

In Genesis 1:27, creation as male and female implies that human beings are to relate to one another, for which marriage (Gen. 2:24) is the most definitive human institution. Both male and female are created in God's image, and therefore neither is definitively *the* human being. Humanity is only adequately represented by both sexes. Clearly, because both female and male bear God's image, neither sex is subordinate to the other.

The *relational* aspect of the image of God is that God can communicate with men and women. In Genesis 1:29–30, God speaks directly to them. Because human beings are made in God's image, we can enter into a relationship with God, and in fact, this relationship with God is the highest call of human beings. Jesus, God Incarnate, echoed this with an invitation: "*Love* one another as I have loved you" (John 15:12, italics added) and even goes so far as to call his followers "friends" (John 15:15), indicating how intimate this relationship can be.

To state this a bit more systematically, creation sets up four basic relationships:

1. With God
2. With other human beings
3. With ourselves (implied)
4. With the rest of creation (other animals, plants, and the earth)

The Ten Commandments (found in Exod. 20 and Deut. 5) exemplify these relationships. The first four begin with God: "I am the LORD your God, who brought you out of the land of Egypt, out of the house of slavery; you shall have no other gods before me" (Exod. 20:2–3). As creatures, our essential relationship is with our Creator. As distinct from other creatures, we can return praise to God. (This makes it all the more depressing that we can grab for ourselves the goods of scientific insight—themselves a gift from God—and forget God in the process.)

Next comes our relationship with other human beings, contained in the next six commandments—honoring our father and mother, not murdering, not committing adultery, not stealing, not bearing false witness, and not coveting (Exod. 20:13–17). Jesus put our human and divine relationships more positively with two citations from the Hebrew Scripture: "'You shall love the Lord your God with all your heart, with all your soul, and with all your mind.' This is the greatest and first commandment. And a second is like it: 'You shall love your neighbor as yourself.' On these two commandments hang all the law and prophets" (Matt. 22:37–40).

Incidentally, we need to be careful not to make Jesus' words a commandment of "self-love" ("as yourself"). Healthy "self-image" comes from the God-image in us, but nowhere in the Bible does God command us to love ourselves. Instead Jesus directs us toward loving our neighbor *as we ourselves would like to be loved.* It is a restatement of the Golden Rule, "In everything do to others as you would have them do to you; for this is the law and the prophets" (Matt. 7:12). Nevertheless, we do have an implied relationship with ourselves, which means we can transcend our own limitations through self-reflection. "What am I doing here?" is a question no other animal ponders. And this relationship with ourselves is affected by the other relationships. Calvin put it this way: knowledge of self and God are intertwined (*Institutes,* 1.1.1).

Consequently, I often find myself praying with St. Augustine: "God, always the same, let me know myself, let me know thee" (*Soliloquies,* Book 2.1).

Finally, we have an implied relationship with the rest of creation. For example, the command for a Sabbath involves resting the animals and letting the earth lie fallow (Lev. 25). This relationship with the rest of creation comes directly from Genesis 1:26. Directly after creating human beings, God says to "let them rule" over all animals. This dominion means that human beings are to be representatives of God's ultimate rule. In the ancient Near East, kings constructing statues of themselves, which signified their sovereignty over that area—something like a sign on the Lincoln Tunnel, "Rudolph Giuliani, Mayor of New York." Human dominion (as in Ps. 8:4–6 quoted at the beginning of the chapter) reflects God's care for the creation. For us, dominion means influence and authority. It is also the command to develop science and technology. Certainly, central air conditioning and heating, vaccines against polio and tuberculosis, and abundant supplies of food and water all evidence our dominion over creation. Unfortunately, so do water pollution and greenhouse gases, mountains of discarded consumer goods, and diminishing rain forests. Our ability to influence the earth can be easily verified, but, like any good ruler, we are to use our sovereignty to protect the weak. Certainly, there are times when it would be easier not to have this authority. What king, or even mayor of New York City, has not longed to be simply a normal citizen for a day?

A contrast highlights the significance of the command to dominion. The eminent scholar of world religions, Huston Smith, has underscored the difference between the Old Testament's portrayal of human representation of God's rule and the more laid-back approach of the *Tao Te Ching:*

> Those who would take over the earth
> And shape it to their will
> Never, I notice, succeed.[35]

Unlike the *Tao,* God directs us to shape the earth. On the other hand, the command in Genesis 1 also differs from Taoism in its emphasis that we are to change the world, not to our will, but *for God's purposes.*

The "dominion mandate" (as theologians call it) represents part of a larger theme: when the Bible speaks of *the image of God* in us, it is making distinctions. We are certainly a part of the created order. In this sense, we are animals. And yet this is not a relationship between equals. In some way, though we bear the divine image, humanity and God are clearly different. God is holy. Old Testament passages such as Exodus 20:4–6 specifically prohibit likenesses of God or "graven images" for this reason. So it is a shock that, as part of our very nature as human beings, we bear a God-likeness.

The teaching of *the image of God* emphasizes the spiritual dimension of human existence. It might lead us to two errors: splitting body and soul and separating us from the rest of creation. Genesis 2 balances Genesis 1 by emphasizing our link with the rest of creation and our essential embodied nature. It uses a wordplay: "Then the Lord God took dust (Hebrew, *adamah*) from the ground and formed *adam* from it" (v. 7, my translation). Being human thus involves both spiritual and material dimensions. To present one to the exclusion of the other distorts our humanity. It is like trying to use one blade of a scissors without the other. It is like a physicist speaking about light without pointing to both its wave and particle characteristics. It is like describing Jesus Christ without underlining *both* his divine and human dimensions.

The New Testament adds some electrifying insights to what Genesis teaches about the image of God. It emphasizes more specifically *the image of Christ* and his work in redeeming the image of God in us. How? Since God is not directly visible to any human beings, we have a tendency to worship created things in the form of idols, because we can see them. Paul opens his magisterial Letter to the Romans with an august and sweeping description of our dire condition. In it he writes not only of first-century idolatry but also of human history generally, "[T]hey exchanged the truth about God for a lie and worshiped and served the creature rather than the Creator, who is blessed forever! Amen" (Rom. 1:25). Nevertheless, Christ has altered this situation, by presenting visibly what eyes cannot see. No one can see God, but Jesus Christ is "the image of the invisible God" (Col. 1:15).

The incarnation of God in Christ also implies a profound truth for human beings: because we bear the image of God, God came to earth in human form. Jesus Christ is fully God and fully man. Thus, Christ has made God fully visible and, in case his readers might be confused, Paul writes in Colossians 2:9, "For in him [Christ] the whole fullness of deity dwells bodily."

Finally, bearing the image of God has a vector toward the future. God will perfect the image of God in us. Christians await Christ's return when Christ's renewed image will be fully realized. First Corinthians 15:49 states the hope of full redemption: "Just as we have borne the image of the man of dust, we will also bear the image of the man of heaven." This aspect of God's creation will be raised again in the final chapter on the end times or eschatology.

Christ, the Image, and Darwin

Christian theology places us as the crown of creation, distinguished from all other animals by God's image. For many centuries, the existence of the intricately designed world offered compelling proof of a Designer. The eighteenth-century philosophical theologian William Paley presented the most enduring image, which he synchronized with Newton's mechanistic worldview. If we found a watch in the middle of a forest, we would not assume it was created by accident. Instead we would conclude there was a watchmaker. The universe is designed with infinitely more intricacy and complexity than a watch. Therefore we are right to determine that there is a Designer.

But the nineteenth century found these conclusions increasingly suspect. Although David Hume's posthumous 1776 *Dialogues Concerning Natural Religion* had preceded Paley, intellectuals ultimately judged Hume as presenting devastating critiques to Paley's watchmaker God. Among various arguments, Hume presented two central ripostes: creation resembles an organism more than a mechanism, and the presence of evil presents a strong argument for disorder rather than order. Natural science followed soon after. Charles Darwin's 1859 *Origin of Species* offered natural selection as a mechanism that needed no Designer. The disappearance of God pulled down humankind with it. Darwin's 1871 *Descent of Man* declared that we are just one more animal, not even a particularly exemplary one at times. And so, it is unsurprising that the twentieth-century atheist and philosophical titan Bertrand Russell could state bluntly: "[M]an is the product of causes which had no prevision of the end they were achieving."[36]

Offering a doctrine of creation in this environment presents a formidable task. It requires that I go back to the history that brings us to this place. The twin forces of philosophical naturalism—nature is the whole story, and there is no God—and Darwinian evolution combined to bring about what the contemporary writer Ian Wilson calls "the funeral of God." Christians clearly cannot believe both naturalism and Darwinism, but can we have one without the other?

Naturalism certainly cannot be the final word for Christians who believe in the God who is greater than the natural world. Some contrast naturalism with *supernaturalism,* a term that takes the Latin *super* meaning "above" and speaks of another reality "above," "beyond," and "greater than" nature. This is fine as long the term does not also bring out the more popular meaning of "the supernatural," with its emphasis on ghosts, demons, and Ouija boards. I will return to naturalism in a moment.

But defining *evolution* presents a trickier problem. What do we mean by the word? Interestingly, Darwin only used the term "evolved" once in his first book because he wanted to avoid its connotations of a predictable unfolding. Darwin emphasized the unpredictable character of change in nature. By his 1872 *Expression of Emotions,* however, he clearly used it. So evolution has stuck with Darwinianism. A few citations from *Origin of Species* provide the core of his theory.

> Owing to the struggle for life, any variation, however slight and from whatever cause proceeding, if it be to any degree profitable to an individual of any species, in its infinitely complex relations to other organic beings and to external nature, will tend to the preservation of that individual, and will generally be inherited by its offspring.

The preservation of favourable variations and the rejection of injurious variations, I call Natural Selection. Variations neither useful nor injurious would not affected be by natural selection, and would be left a fluctuating element.

It follows that as each selected and favoured form increases in number, so will the less favoured forms decrease and become rare. Rarity, as geology tells us, is the precursor to extinction.

According to my view, varieties are species in the process of formation, or, as I have called them, incipient species.[37]

Many of these statements about Darwinism are familiar from high school biology. Kenneth Miller, the Brown University biologist, summarizes the mechanisms of evolution succinctly: mutation, variation, and natural selection.[38]

But what theological conclusions did Darwin, this erstwhile student of theology, draw from his theories? The answer may offer some clue about the metaphysical implications of evolution. Darwin seems to have preferred the God of deism who simply brings the world into motion and then steps back, preferring not to interact with humankind:

There is grandeur in this view of life; with its several powers having been originally breathed by the Creator into a few forms or into one; and that, whilst this planet has gone cycling on according to the fixed law of gravity, from so simple a beginning endless forms most wonderful and beautiful have been, and are being evolved.[39]

So Darwin, at least, drew the conclusion that these processes led to a deity unlike the one described by orthodox Christianity. The later disciples of his theory have often taken this conclusion further and found a deistic god scientifically unnecessary and personally uninteresting.

To some degree, the religious implications of his theories delayed Darwin in publishing his work for at least fifteen years. He was not a man drawn to disputes. But that was not the only cause. Darwin knew he also lacked two major scientific elements: sufficient geological age and a specific mechanism for evolution.

Nineteenth-century scientists did not find the sun to be old enough. The imposing Lord Kelvin, admitted to the University of Glasgow at ten and appointed to a professorship there at twenty-two, pronounced that the sun had shined for no more than five hundred million years. This period was longer than Bishop Ussher's famous calculation that the earth began on the night before 23 October 4004 B.C., but not long enough for evolution. Fortunately for Darwin's theory—but not for Darwin, who had already died—later discoveries of radioactivity led to the conclusion that the sun had been in business for five billion years. Darwinism found new life.

In 1866 the work of the monk, botanist, and first geneticist, Gregor Mendel, offered evolution a specific mechanism, although his discoveries only became widely known at the end of nineteenth century. Mendel's work demonstrated that specific traits in plants can be passed on. In other words, he had discovered the gene. Further refinements in genetics in the early twentieth century culminated in 1953 when, in their own recounting, Francis Crick and James D. Watson burst into the Eagle, a pub in Cambridge, England, and declared that they had found the secret of life in the double helix of DNA. Here the essentially digital sequencing of four nucleotide bases A, C, G, T (adenosine, cytosine, guanine, and thymine) creates a code for life. Advances in genetics have certainly not stopped, but in recent years have produced the mapping of the entire human genetic structure in the Human Genome Project, the breakthroughs in animal cloning, and the use of DNA analysis in the courtroom.

Genetics and evolutionary theory were brought together in the middle of the twentieth century in a systematic neo-Darwinism. Contemporary evolutionary scientists utilize a variety of disciplines such as biology, statistics, and genetics to formulate specific conclusions. They speak of the current human being, Homo sapiens, emerging approximately three hundred thousand years ago, preceded by earlier forms of humanlike creatures, which appeared three hundred million years ago, themselves preceded by dinosaurs who ruled the earth for millions of years, and ultimately resting on single-cell organisms about three billion years ago. All of this is familiar to students of evolutionary theory.

Recent neo-Darwinians Stephen Jay Gould, Daniel Dennett, and Richard Dawkins are not content with scientific discovery and theory alone, but add specifically anti-God elements in their writings. Dawkins is always helpful in this regard because he continually uses evolutionary theory to bludgeon believers. His brilliance and bluntness combine in even one sample: "The more you understand the significance of evolution, the more you are pushed away from the agnostic position and towards atheism."[40] Nevertheless, the basic elements of evolution are quite spare and not nearly so metaphysical.

As I mentioned above, Darwin knew his theories would provoke theological controversy. If the creation of human beings is the process of a lengthy evolutionary process, it is difficult to conclude that Adam and Eve were historical figures. Darwin particularly feared that he would be accused of the "murder of Adam," and this fear also delayed the publication of his theories.

One might expect that theologians immediately responded in dismay, finding their literary readings of Genesis 1 threatened. The standard history tells of a meeting of the British Association for the Advancement of Science in 1860. There the Bishop of Oxford, Samuel Wilberforce, questioned Darwin's champion, T. H. Huxley, as to whether he claimed descent from monkeys on his grandfather's or grandmother's side. Huxley is reported to have replied:

> A man has no reason to be ashamed of having an ape for his grandfather. If there were an ancestor whom I should feel shame in recalling it would be a *man*—a man of restless and versatile intellect—who, not content with success in his own sphere of activity, plunges into scientific questions with which he has no real acquaintance, only to obscure them by an aimless rhetoric, and distract the attention of his hearers from the real point at issue by eloquent digressions and skilled appeals to religious prejudice.[41]

Despite the fact that this story finds its way into many popular histories of science, recent research shows that the final form of this exchange took shape long after the events themselves and probably received some embellishment. Even more to the point, Wilberforce presided at that meeting of the association as vice president and presented his objections to Darwinism as a scientist. As I've pointed out, the *scientific* argument for Darwinism left many questions unanswered—it was entirely possible to argue against Darwinism on a scientific basis.

Others look to the American example of a theologically based prejudice against Darwinism: the 1925 Dayton, Tennessee, "Monkey Trial" of John Scopes for teaching evolution. Facing off for the prosecution was the orator and politician William Jennings Bryan. For the defense stood the greatest trial lawyer of the day, Clarence Darrow. Truth and freedom on trial against superstition, right? This has only been reinforced by the movie *Inherit the Wind,* which adds its own legendary elements to present science as the defender of truth and religion as the patron of ignorance. Again the actual facts are more complicated. Scopes, a physical education teacher and substitute teacher in biology, was put forward by the American Civil Liberties Union to test the recently passed state law that forbade the teaching of evolution. (Later Scopes told reporters that he was unsure that he ever taught evolution.) Although he lost the case, the judgment was later reversed on technical grounds, and ultimately public opinion declared Scopes the winner. Certainly Bryan was ignorant of many points of evolution, which became painfully obvious when he foolishly took the stand to be devastatingly cross-examined by Darrow. Nevertheless, many prominent scientists at the time, such as Arthur Smith Woodward, Arthur Keith, and Grafton Elliot Smith, would not have fared much better, since they held to the authenticity of Piltdown man ("ancient human fossils" that later turned out to be a fraud) as evidence of their theories. Clearly this case should not exemplify a serious confrontation between religion and science nor a serious theological assessment of the impact of evolution.

In fact, the early theological response spanned all the way from outright rejection to enthusiastic adulation. Henry Drummond found an impressive coherence between evolution and the Christian faith.

> What is evolution? A method of creation. What is its object? To make more perfect beings. What is Christianity? A method of creation. What is its object? To make more perfect living beings.

> Through what does Evolution work? Through love. Through
> what does Christianity work? Through love. Evolution and
> Christianity have the same author, the same end, the same
> spirit.[42]

This response seems surprisingly naive and would have horrified
Drummond's contemporary, the doyen of the late-nineteenth-
century "Princeton Theology," Charles Hodge. Hodge rejected
Darwinism because it led to design by an impersonal force and
thus the elimination of God. (This charge, curiously, is enthusias-
tically endorsed a century later by Dawkins and by the Intelligent
Design movement.) Hodge declared, "The conclusion of the whole
matter is, that the denial of design in nature is virtually the denial
of God. . . . What is Darwinism? It is Atheism."[43]

In recent years, the Intelligent Design movement has taken on
evolution and has provoked some stirring debate about the truth of
Darwin's theory. Because ID (as it is often referred to) criticizes
Darwinism vigorously at points, some conflate it with the more
antievolution stance of young-earth creationists. ID, however, represents a broad coalition of perspectives that reflects a more
nuanced critique of Darwinism with three major points:

1. The intricate design of creation points to an intelligent
   Designer. (Thus the movement's name.)
2. Neo-Darwinism is inherently atheistic and materialistic.
3. Darwinism cannot be sustained on scientific grounds because
   of the relative paucity of transitional forms (for example).

To the first, I agree and will unfold the reasons in the next section.
I agree—as long as we say that creation *witnesses* to God's existence, but does not *prove* it. To the second, I would say that many
contemporary evolutionists are atheistic and use their theories to
propagandize. I am still shocked by Dawkins, who asserts that if
critics find any problems with Darwinism—and his atheism as
well—they are blinded by religion. "In most cases, they know
deep down what to believe because their parents recommended an
ancient book that tells them what to believe."[44] This surprises me
since I have problems with atheistic evolution, although I never

learned the Bible in my family. That we must believe in Dawkins's worldview is clearly not true. One can consider the example of the head of the Human Genome Project, Francis Collins, who was converted to Christianity in medical school.

On the third point, ID points to some incriminating quotes, like Gould's statement, "The extreme rarity of transitional forms in the fossil record persists as the trade secret of paleontology,"[45] or Darwin's own concession that his theory was "grievously hypothetical."[46] ID raises interesting problems and provokes a response from evolutionists that is more visceral than substantive. Nevertheless, many Christian scientists find evolution compelling, and most scientists believe this movement has exaggerated the problems with neo-Darwinian theory. For example, Gould continues in the citation above by asserting a punctuated, rather than gradual, form of evolution. Neo-Darwinian evolutionary theory still produces fruitfulness in a wide range of fields, and is based on considerable evidence. Unfortunately, ID has not yet presented a convincing alternative case. Perhaps the day is to come, but for now, many Christians believe that evolution and Christianity are compatible.

Can one believe in the scientific merit of evolution without its naturalism and thus atheism? Yes. I agree with the Presbyterian Church (U.S.A.)'s affirmation: "Neither Scripture, our Confession of Faith, nor our Catechisms, teach the Creation of man by the direct and immediate acts of God so as to exclude the possibility of evolution as a scientific theory."[47]

With this in mind, I make two conclusions in relation to God's creation of humankind. We *must* reject the naturalism of much neo-Darwinism. Most important, it cannot become a substitute religion, although it seems to function this way for many scientists. In this respect, Dawkins sounds as shrill as the most overenthusiastic evangelist. Consider the evangelistic notes in his introduction to *The Blind Watchmaker* and broad applications for this theory:

> Darwinism encompasses all of life—human, animal, plant, bacterial, and, if I am right in the last chapter of this book, extraterrestrial. It provides *the only satisfying explanation* for why we all exist, why we are the way that we are. It is the bedrock on which rest all the disciplines known as the humanities.[48]

Relegating Dawkins to a slim minority would be comforting, but unfortunately his position finds echoes in similar statements by Gould, Crick, and Dennett. Certainly Christians cannot hold to this form of naturalistic evolution.

On the other hand, one can certainly believe that God, who is greater than the boundaries of space and time, is free to choose the means of creating humankind. We must avoid the following argument: God does what is best. We know (and propose) the best way for God to create. Therefore we know that God has created in this way. Instead, the great Christian scientists like Newton, Kepler, Galileo, and Maxwell have all looked seriously at the evidence of God's creation and made their conclusions accordingly. A scientist and member of my church once lamented, "They're atheist, and they have the best science!" Or to paraphrase a quote attributed to Martin Luther about music, "Why should the Devil have all the good science?"

Contemporary scientists have concluded that both microevolution (the changes within existing species) and macroevolution (the formation of a new species altogether) have solid support. Accepting the latter, however, implies that the image of God in women and men probably emerged over time. It is certainly possible that God uniquely and specially created the particular creature Adam, and this conclusion cannot be strictly proved or disproved by science. Nonetheless, current evolutionary theory more strongly supports that God used secondary causes to form human beings. Neither method—a direct, special creation or a transition from earlier life forms—greatly changes our understanding of God's creation of humankind. Either way God created us with a particular ability to respond and to seek a relationship with our Creator. Similarly, God has given us the responsibility of living ethically in light of our relationship to others and to all creation. In addition, our intelligence and perception of the fine-tuning of the universe constitute key elements in our special place in the created order. Put another way, neo-Darwinism does not alter the fundamental theological commitment to relationality as the essence of bearing God's image. If God's image came through the evolutionary process, this fact merely extends the time for its development in us.

How then can we look at Genesis 1 and 2 as twenty-first-century Christians? Clearly, the primary concern of these texts is not contemporary scientific questions. *Their main intention is to describe the creation of an ordered and habitable home for the people God creates.* Thus, many contemporary readers find a constrictive literalism inadequate for understanding these texts. For example, seven twenty-four-hour days of creation do not make sense in terms of contemporary cosmological theory. In 1000 B.C., no reader or hearer (since very few read at that time) could understand contemporary quantum cosmology or neo-Darwinian theory. Accordingly, theologians have spoken of God's *accommodation:* that the revelation of God accommodates itself to the understanding of human minds. Calvin, writing at the time of major scientific changes in the sixteenth century, put it similarly: "Moses wrote in a popular style things which, without instruction, all ordinary persons endued with common sense, are liable to understand."[49]

Do these texts fade behind the brilliance of scientific insight? Hardly. They still radiate great power and wisdom as foundational texts for the Christian church, as sparkling insights into ours and God's nature. One might even view it as an act of providence that these biblical texts, written long before the emergence of modern science, resonate with certain contemporary scientific theories in the texts.

First of all, Genesis 1:3—"Let there be light"—initiates a sequence of events with the sudden emergence of light, similar to the unparalleled outburst of energy in the Big Bang. Indeed light comes first, and reminds me of the fundamental constant in Einstein's special relativity theory, the velocity of light. (Einstein emphasized this absolute standard. Wanting to avoid any hint of relativism, he promoted the term *Invarententheorie,* "invariance theory." His attempt to name his theory failed, and "relativity" stuck.) In addition, light was created before our sun, which came billions of years after the initial singularity of the Big Bang.

Second, the order of water, vegetation, nonhuman animals, and then humankind in Genesis 1:6–31 has a broad agreement with the sequence of life's emergence in evolutionary theory. In addition, the command "Let the earth put forth vegetation" speaks of an indirect creation by God. Science describes a universe of continuity, where God creates humankind *indirectly* through the processes of nature over time. Put in philosophical terms, God as the First Cause uses *secondary* causes to achieve divine purposes.

Third, and in a similar vein, evolutionary theory does not necessarily change God's creating us, but simply the means God uses. The declaration of Genesis 2:7, "[T]hen the LORD God formed man from the dust of the ground, and breathed into his nostrils the breath of life," depicts with great consonance the creation of man and woman. Once again, extreme literalism will not do: dust does not contain enough carbon nor usually sufficient silicon.

Kenneth Miller, a biologist who combines a commitment to evolutionary science with his Christian faith, argues against such literalism and for a sensible reading of the texts:

> To any biochemist, even an evolutionary biochemist, the notion that human life was formed from the dust of the earth is not only poetic, but scientifically accurate to an astonishing degree. An extreme literalist—of the sort abjured by Augustine—might use Genesis 2:7 to argue that the elemental composition of the human body should *match* that of ordinary dust. A broader and more sensible reading would tell us simply that the materials of the human body were taken from the earth itself, which of course is true. To understand Genesis, to find the greater truth, I would argue, all one has to do is to apply the more sensible reading throughout.[50]

A sensible or "natural" reading (to use Calvin's term) is a good rule of thumb. In this case, it leads to striking parallels with contemporary science. Nevertheless, one must apply such interpretive parallels with a light touch. We will do well not to bet the farm on any particular scientific theory. As the Oxford philosopher Janet Martin Soskice has concluded, Darwinian science did not disprove faith. It simply took on the watchmaker God of the eighteenth century—which incidentally neither Calvin, Augustine, nor Jesus ever presented—and demonstrated its insufficiency as description of God's character. Soskice writes that

> *because* the theological apologetics of the eighteenth century had been so closely wedded to the science of their time, with its

support for the arguments from design, the controversies over evolutionary theory came in the nineteenth century as a powerful blow. Religion's dearest ally had turned on it. Science, which had been proving the truths of religion only a hundred years before, now proposed naturalistic explanations for the perfections and order of the natural world. The divine clockmaker was redundant.[51]

So, too, I turn to a surprising set of scientific discoveries known as the anthropic principle with caution. Nevertheless, here we find impressive scientific support for belief in God the Creator.

The Anthropic Principle

Since the 1960s, scientists have turned up astonishing findings that the universe has certain, very specific conditions that allow for the emergence of conscious, moral creatures. This set of discoveries offers compelling evidence for a Designer. The anthropic principle derives its name from the Greek word for "human being," *anthropos,* and simply states that the universe is fitted from its inception for the emergence of life in general and intelligent life in particular. Ian Barbour, whose work represents the foundation of most who labor in the field of science and theology, has outlined three elements that characterize the anthropic principle:[52]

1. *The Expansion Rate:* Stephen Hawking has written, "If the rate of expansion after the Big Bang had been smaller by even one part in a hundred thousand million it would have recollapsed before its present size." On the other hand, if it had been greater by one part in a million, the universe would have expanded too rapidly for stars and planets to form.
2. *The Formation of the Elements:* If the strong nuclear force had been even slightly weaker, we would have had only hydrogen in the universe. If the force had been even slightly stronger, all the hydrogen would have been converted to helium. In either case, stable stars and compounds such as water could not have formed. Similarly, the nuclear force is only barely sufficient for carbon to form; yet if it had been slightly stronger, the carbon would all have been converted

into oxygen. The element carbon has many properties that are crucial to the later development of organic life as we know it.

3. *The Particle/Antiparticle Ratio:* For every billion antiprotons in the early universe, there were one billion and one protons. The billion pairs annihilated each other to produce radiation, with just one proton left over. A greater or smaller number of survivors—or no survivors at all (if they had been evenly matched)—would have made our kind of material world impossible.

Barbour then adds, "The simultaneous occurrence of many independent improbable features appears *wildly* improbable."[53] In fact, one can go further: physicists have identified over thirty discrete, precisely calibrated parameters that produced the universe we know. Even one of these parameters could be described as "wildly improbable." Oxford physicist Roger Penrose comments that the "phase-space volume" requires a meticulous fine-tuning such that the "Creator's aim must have been [precise] to an accuracy of one part in $10^{10^{123}}$"—a number almost impossible to write: 1 followed by 10^{123} zeroes.[54]

Are these factors just the result of an exceedingly improbable chance, or are they the design plans of God? To argue the case for a random, accidental emergence of life appears to be an unwarranted leap of faith. Much simpler is the conclusion that a Creator designed the universe with the emergence of conscious, moral life in mind. Freeman Dyson, the physicist who has spent his recent years at Princeton's famed Institute for Advanced Study, collected the Templeton Prize for the Advancement of Religion in 1999. He commented, "The more I examine the universe and the details of its architecture, the more evidence I find that the universe in some sense must have known we were coming."[55] Indeed, Stephen Hawking, the man who holds Isaac Newton's former chair at Cambridge and wears his symbolic mantle as well, has written, "The odds against a universe like ours out of something like the Big Bang are enormous. I think there are clearly religious implications."[56]

What exactly are these implications? Christianity has taught the importance of humans as self-conscious creatures who can return praise and worship God. For this reason, we are the "crown" of creation. (Are we the only beings in the universe capable of conscious response? Given an immensely creative God, extraterrestrial life cannot be ruled out. Still science has no definitive word, and so I will leave speculation aside.) The anthropic principle adds scientific evidence that God created the world out of love for us, in order that we could be in relationship with our Creator. This confirming evidence in the structure of creation appears to be the fingerprint of God.

Yet, we also have to admit that human beings have left another, less benevolent fingerprint as God's representatives on earth.

Ecology and the Doctrine of Creation

The doctrine of creation offered a vision for the early Israelites to live on the earth. But what insights does it offer us, a world of billions who seem poised on ecological apocalypse? Technology, the child of science, has brought with it greenhouse gases, polluted rivers, and bulging landfills. In 1967 the historian Lynn White, of the University of California, Los Angeles, laid down the gauntlet for Christianity, blaming its dominion mandate as the major player in the ecological crisis. White argued that this concept of dominion over nature has led to the West's devaluation of the natural world, exemplified in statements like René Descartes that we are "masters and possessors" of nature. Although he pointed to minor figures in Christianity, such as Francis of Assisi, who presented a more collaborative relationship with the natural world (after all, Francis preached to the birds), White concluded that Christianity bears a "huge burden of guilt" for the present ecological crisis.[57] Similarly, recent theologies have sought to revise or excise the call to dominion, replacing it with a more congenial and symmetrical relationship with nonhuman creation. Some Christian revisionists even veer toward earth worship.

I find these to be overreactions based on misunderstanding. Yet,

White's indictment clearly has much to commend it. Western civilization—that most closely associated with Christianity—has marred the environment. (Although other civilizations have also done their share.) Interestingly, however, this environmental exploitation occurred as our culture became increasingly secularized, at a time when science and capitalism increased in power and religion's influence diminished. Perhaps it is not surprising then that the noted paleontologist and anticreationist Niles Eldridge once allowed the environment as the only topic religion and science can discuss. The *New York Times* reported a comment by Eldridge in 1998, "There's an ecological component to all concepts of God."[58]

In fact, White's insight reveals two significant distortions of Christian doctrine. The call of Genesis 1:26 to *dominion,* though a strong word, is not a call to decimation. We must first read this text in its context. No ancient Israelite could imagine the level of control over the created order that we can now exercise. Still, even in the Bible, dominion is epitomized by the empowering and nurturing of a good king. Just as a good king cares for the needy and marginal, so we should care for a fragile world. Consider the effect of God's spirit falling on the messianic king of Isaiah 11:4. By the spirit of the Lord, "with righteousness he shall judge the poor, and decide with equity for the meek of the earth." Surely, God has given humankind great power. But with power comes responsibility.

In addition, the Reformed tradition continually calls us to *simplicity,* a theological motif that emerged simultaneously with, and as a correction to, protocapitalism. Much of the ecological crisis remains linked to the Western world's excessive materialism. For example, the United States claims less than 5 percent of the world's population and yet accounts for 25 percent of its total energy use. Industries could certainly work toward an ecological business ethic, but this fact also hits close to home. Our apartments and houses create the lion's share of pollution. Leaving lights on, turning thermostats too high, and driving huge gas-guzzling and polluting sport utility vehicles all use energy needlessly. A return to simplicity, and with it a "greening" of our lives, would be both a sign of holy living and a means of preserving our planet.

Love: Created for Community

Love is the primary virtue that corresponds to creation in God's image. This love is best exemplified by Jesus Christ and awakened in us by the Holy Spirit. "We love because [God] first loved us" (1 John 4:19). The image of God and the love it evokes flow into all human relationships. The metaphor of the church as Christ's body (as in Eph. 4:12) gives this ethical dimension a social emphasis. As I will highlight in the next chapter, the image of God in all women and men leads to a deep respect for human dignity. Put negatively, James 3:9 says that to curse other people and praise God is unthinkable since we "are made in the likeness of God." Because men and women are made in God's image, they have dignity and are to be respected, no matter how poverty, social injustice, and bad personal decisions have defaced this image. The slang is right: "God don't make no junk."

As bearers of the image of God, we have the place of highest honor and responsibility in all creation. The tragedy of evil is that it defaces the divine image. The glory of Christ's work is its restoration of God's image in us. Our highest calling is to reflect God's image in Christ.

We are therefore created for community . . . or maybe better, for Holy Communion. The sacrament of the Lord's Supper celebrates our relationship with God and with one another. It also employs the basic products of the earth (bread and wine), sanctifying them and carrying with them God's presence. Through this sacrament, we restore our relationship with God, with our community, with the earth, and with ourselves. In a word, we are healed. In Communion, the Risen Christ clarifies and polishes God's image in us. Through this sacrament, the Great Artist continues to refashion us as a cherished creation. Vincent van Gogh, in a letter to his brother Theo, expressed beautifully this assurance: "Christ . . . is more of an artist than the artists; he works in the living spirit and the living flesh; he makes human beings instead of statues."[59]

4

Everything's Not Right with the World: Evil, the Fall, and Yet Providence

So when the woman saw that the tree was good for food, and that it was a delight to the eyes, and that the tree was to be desired to make one wise, she took of its fruit and ate; and she also gave some to her husband, who was with her, and he ate.

Then the eyes of both were opened, and they knew that they were naked; and they sewed fig leaves together and made loincloths for themselves. . . .

And the LORD God made garments of skins for the man and for his wife, and clothed them.

Genesis 3:6–7, 21

If we regard the Spirit of God as the sole fountain of truth, we shall neither reject the truth itself, nor despise it wherever it shall appear, unless we wish to dishonor the Spirit of God.

John Calvin

Through many dangers, toils, and snares I have already come;
'Tis grace has brought me safe thus far, and grace will lead me home.

John Newton, "Amazing Grace"

God is good and created the world good. Yet there is evil. Clearly there is a difficulty here. And this problem of evil and suffering has plagued thinkers throughout history as they tried to reconcile the existence of an all-powerful, all-knowing, benevolent God with the reality of evil. The mathematician-philosopher Alfred North Whitehead summarized it aptly:

"All simplifications of religious dogma are shipwrecked upon the rock of the problem of evil."[60]

The Reality and Nature of Evil

Richard Dawkins thinks he has the answer to the problem of evil—simply remove God. In *River out of Eden* (it is curious how obsessed he is with biblical images), he describes the crashing of a school bus with Roman Catholic children aboard. Following the accident, theologians wrestled with God's goodness in light of these needless deaths. This Oxford evolutionary scientist subtly mocks their intellectual pains, essentially responding that if there is no God, there is no problem.

> If the universe were just electrons and selfish genes, meaningless tragedies like the crashing of a bus are exactly what we should expect, along with equally meaningless *good* fortune. Such a universe would be neither evil nor good in intention. It would manifest no intentions of any kind. In a universe of blind physical forces and genetic replication, some people are going to get hurt, other people are going to get lucky, and you won't find any rhyme or reason in it, nor any justice. The universe that we observe has precisely the properties we should expect if there is, at bottom, no design, no purpose, no evil and no good, nothing but blind, pitiless indifference.
>
> As the unhappy poet A. E. Housman put it:
> For Nature, heartless, witless Nature
> Will neither know nor care.
> DNA neither knows nor cares. DNA just is. And we dance to its music.[61]

I am amazed by Dawkins's willingness to lay his cards on the table. He admits that atheistic materialism leads to a life evacuated of meaning. A gracious God who comforts and protects is displaced by the control of godlike but heartless DNA. Dawkins finds a way to solve the problem of evil and suffering by removing meaning from these events. Yet, to remove God adds the problem of good. Why should good exist without a beneficent Creator? It is certainly a Pyrrhic victory. Besides his stunning admission, there is something heartless and dehumanizing about his response. To say that this sort of tragedy poses no problem strikes me as unrelentingly cruel. Christianity sees things differently. As we know God more and more, we do not construct easy answers for pain and suffering—we become increasingly sensitive to it.

Nevertheless many today—whether scientists or not—conclude that the reality of evil and suffering present insurmountable challenges to belief in a benevolent deity. They present evolution as indisputable evidence. In place of the good Creator, Dawkins proffers DNA, the "blind watchmaker." Darwinian evolution directs natural processes. We are left with nature evacuated of God's grandeur and marked "red with tooth and claw."

I want to pause there. I find evolutionists' atheism—based on natural evil—extremely curious. No one living before Darwin would have been surprised to hear that evil exists. Job 14:1–2 puts it so well:

> A mortal, born of woman, few of days and full of trouble,
>   comes up like a flower and withers,
>   flees like a shadow and does not last.

The recognition of evil's reality far preceded the development of modern science—and particularly Darwin's theories. What has changed is our civilization's stance toward God: Job seeks to argue with God, but finds himself ultimately bowing before divine authority and grandeur. In contrast, we live a time in which we stand in judgment of God. We no longer fear whether God has enough evidence to condemn us. Instead we prosecute a case against God.

This fact by itself does not make the problems go away. It does, however, remind us of the peculiarities of this moment in history. It can offer perspective as we approach the following questions: Is the world rendered meaningless by the presence of evil? Does evil make God unbelievable? The response to these questions thankfully does not depend on the current climate.

"I stood already to the profound duplicity of life, that humankind is not truly one but two. And that these polar twins should be continuously struggling." So begins Robert Louis Stevenson's famous *Dr. Jekyll and Mr. Hyde.* The Bible also expresses quite clearly that everything is not right with us and our world. The world does not perfectly reflect God's character. It may be good, but it is not perfect. Human dignity, so definitively imprinted in God's image, does not represent the whole story. If I left the discussion simply at the last chapter, an unrealistic picture of humankind in its glory emerges. We know human violence, betrayal, and daily petty barbarism. (Have you ridden a subway in New York City?) Genesis 3 describes Adam and Eve's moving away, a "falling," from perfection. Though we may not be literally as divided as Dr. Jekyll and Mr. Hyde—who performed scientific experiments and cavorted with the English gentry by day and then murdered under the cloak of night—we do demonstrate a mix of cruelty and dignity. We bear not only the image of God, but the marks of evil.

What then is evil and its sibling, sin?

Outside the church, people often think of sin and temptation in terms of sex. This is far from the biblical view. In fact, the first mention of sexuality, Adam's "becoming one flesh" with Eve, only has connotations of intimacy and joy. Sin is an abuse of freedom that distorts God's gifts to us by using them wrongly. Nevertheless, our culture is hung up on sex. It often reduces sin to sex and then presents it as irresistible temptation—especially if it can sell a product. Coiled somewhere around our cultural memory lies the deceitful serpent in the Garden of Eden. This image, of the snake tempting Eve with an apple (the exact fruit belongs to John Milton and not Genesis), has stunning durability. In the late summer of 2000, I walked to work down Fifth Avenue, passing the Henri Bendel store. A magnificent display for the "Temptress Collection" by Laura Mercier Cosmetics included a coiled snake with a pile of apples. The implicit message was that temptation equals sexuality (which then equals sales for Laura Mercier).

But the Bible sees things quite differently. Evil in Scripture is anything that brings sorrow, distress, or calamity, including moral evil in which we choose to hurt one another or any part of creation. Evil seeks to thwart the life-giving power of God and thus God's will. Sin is a related term. Sin effects evil. It is the human condition of separation from God and has the particularly religious connotations of breaking God's law, failing God's will, or actively rebelling against God. In most cases, "sin" and "moral evil" can be used interchangeably. (I suspect that if "sin" has any meaning to those outside the church—besides overindulging in sex and or eating a "sinful chocolate cake"—it means what I would call moral evil.) The ultimate sin is idolatry: to reject the one, true, living God and to put anything in God's place. But there is more: Sin also has a "directional" quality. Whereas natural processes may effect evil as a byproduct (for example, rain causes both crops to grow and rivers to flood), sin is directed toward producing harm. In addition, the New Testament (for example, Rom. 7:13–25) sometimes personifies sin. In these cases, sin encompasses the cosmic, demonic structures and powers that promote evil. Behind all sin and evil lie these mysterious cosmic dimensions. Here I will emphasize the human scale and will primarily describe evil.

There was a day—just two centuries ago—when we, as a culture, were so optimistic about inherent human goodness that we defined evil as ignorance. If we knew more, the better (morally) we would be. This intoxicating optimism enjoyed an "Indian summer" in the late nineteenth century. World War I shocked Western civilization from its stupor. The most advanced "Christian" nations of the Western world were killing each other through the horrors of chemical warfare. Subsequently, the Nazi death camps, the nuclear horrors of Hiroshima and Nagasaki, and later the growing problems of overpopulation, intransigent racism, ecological destruction, and worldwide disease, and now global terrorism have cured humankind of this illusion. The existence of evil did not surprise the biblical writers, who clearly saw that evil clings to human existence. As Paul declares, "So I find it to be a law that when I want to do what is good, evil lies close at hand" (Rom. 7:21).

The Old Testament does not distinguish between moral evil and calamity in its terminology for evil. Some basic meanings for evil are sadness (Gen. 44:34), danger (as in the "dangerous animals" of Lev. 26:6), grievous ill (Eccl. 6:2), and wickedness (1 Sam. 12:17).

The most important definition of evil is a rejection of God's way and law (Deut. 4:25; 1 Kgs. 11:6; 2 Kgs. 21:2; see Heb. 3:12). The problem with the reality of evil originates from the fundamental biblical confession that God created a good world. In Genesis, we read both that God declares the world "good" and "very good," and yet that evil lurks in the background of creation as a chaos that threatens the order of creation. "The earth was a formless void and darkness covered the face of the deep" (Gen. 1:2). Here also lurks the problem of evil in the world: If God has created the heaven and earth good, why does evil persist? In this sense, every brother who dies of a heart attack, every soul that dies rejecting God, every person killed by an earthquake or tsunami presents one more argument against the existence of a good, all-powerful God. At times the presence of evil in the creation is so pervasive that "the world" becomes associated with the realm of evil. For instance, even though the Gospel of John clearly indicates that God created the world (John 1:10), it also emphasizes that "the world" is now a place largely in rebellion against its Creator (John 12:31; 15:19). Still, John never describes evil as greater than the good that is in creation: "The light shines in the darkness, and the darkness did not overcome it" (John 1:5).

There is no extended discussion in the Bible for why evil exists in the world. Nonetheless, *freedom*—the gift to men and women that offers us the potential for true relationships—plays a significant part in the entrance of evil into the Garden in Genesis 3. In Genesis 2:16–17, God commands the man to eat from any tree, except "of the tree of the knowledge of good and evil." Theologians for centuries have debated the meaning of this tree, but what is most important here for understanding evil is that, from the beginning, human beings are given free choices. We are given the power to select from many good alternatives and an ability to disobey—freedom to enter into relationships and freedom to break them. So, when the woman and man eat from this tree, they have abused their freedom and severed their relationship with God. This rupture is captured in that chilling question God poses, "Where are you?" (Gen. 3:9), as Adam is found hiding from God. God does curse them, bringing pain to Eve in childbirth, subjugation to her husband, toil in Adam's work, and alienation in his relationship with the earth (Gen. 3:16–19). Nevertheless, after this bad choice, God demonstrates care for them by making clothes of animal skins for them, a necessity that signifies the distance between human and nonhuman creation (v. 21). Put simply, Genesis 3 teaches that evil enters from an abuse of freedom.

Many have also mined the book of Job for gems of insight into the presence of evil and the existence of a good God. Job 1:6–12 begins by describing Satan (or "the adversary"), who is responsible for the evil that will happen to Job and that God allows (but does not cause). The presence of evil angels (also described in 1 Sam. 16:14–23 and 1 Kgs. 22:19–23) does not solve the problem of the origin of evil. It adds a complexity that behind all earthly powers, there is spiritual realm of evil. The possibility for rebelling against God exists at the cosmic level. There is also a warning in this text to a culture curious about the might of supernatural evil. Satan is never portrayed as an equal to God. God alone controls the universe.

As Job's trials continue, he raises the biblical question of why the righteous (and especially Job!) suffer (Job 16:11; 30:26). The final section of Job (38:1–42:6) offers no definitive answer, except that the suffering of the righteous forms a mysterious part of creation and that God's presence is more important than answers to the questions evil raises.

> Then the LORD answered Job out of the whirlwind:
> "Who is this that darkens counsel by words without knowledge?
> Gird up your loins like a man,
>   I will question you, and you shall declare to me.
>
> Where were you when I laid the foundation of the earth?
>   Tell me, if you have understanding.
> Who determined its measurements—surely you know!
>   Or who stretched the line upon it?
> On what were its bases sunk,
>   Or who laid its cornerstone
> when the morning stars sang together
>   and all the heavenly beings shouted for joy?"
>   (Job 38:1–7)

God concludes by speaking of the great mythical sea monster, Leviathan—a beast signifying ultimate chaos—with whom simply God plays.

> Can you draw out Leviathan with a fishhook,
>   or press down its tongue with a cord?
> Will you play with it as with a bird,
>   or will you put it on leash for your girls?
>
> (Job 41:1, 5)

Job finds satisfaction in a personal encounter with the Lord, and confesses his ignorance. "Therefore I have uttered what I did not understand, things too wonderful for me which I did not know" (42:3). He repents in dust and ashes, a sign of his fragile humanity. In other words, when it comes to the mystery of evil, it is not about us, but about God. And mystery may have the final word.

For all its insight, Job does not exhaust the Old Testament's reflections on the presence of evil. Two additional responses are noteworthy:

1. God's will is not thwarted by evil, but God can take evil and transform its wreckage into something good. As Joseph said to his brothers who had sold him into slavery, "Even though you intended to do harm to me, God intended it for good, in order to preserve a numerous people, as he is doing today" (Gen. 50:20).
2. Sin may satisfy in the short term, but it fails in the long term because its separates us from the greatest good, God.

> Indeed, those who are far from you will perish;
>   you put an end to those who are false to you.
> But . . . I have made the Lord GOD my refuge.
>   to tell of all your works.
>
> (Ps. 73:27–28)

The New Testament understands evil in the same way that the Old Testament does—as both moral wrong and calamity—but adds some new insights. First of all, it affirms that God is not responsible for evil. James 1:13 expresses it simply: "God cannot be tempted by evil and he himself tempts no one." Though evil exists in the world, it can never overcome good (John 1:5). In the Lord's Prayer, Jesus instructs his disciples to pray that God would "deliver us from evil" (traditional rendering), implying that God is greater than evil. As God does, so we do: Christians are encouraged never to repay evil for evil (Rom. 12:17), but actively to resist it in their own behavior. Third John 11 puts it similarly: "Beloved, do not imitate what is evil but imitate what is good."

The cross of Christ transforms the Christian understanding of evil and offers the central theological element to any theological response to evil: Jesus, the very Son of God, died at the hands of evil men and women. God has overcome evil by suffering in Jesus. As 1 Peter 2:23–24 sets out,

> When he was abused, he did not return abuse; when he suffered, he did not threaten; but he entrusted himself to the one who judges justly. He himself bore our sins in his body on the cross, so that, free from sins, we might live for righteousness; by his wounds you have been healed.

God is not far off from human struggle with evil. Instead, Jesus, God in human flesh, has taken on evil.

Evil surrounds us every moment of our lives. Reflection on the presence of evil has led to the philosophical formulation, "How can a good and all-powerful God create a world with evil in it?" Either God—it seems—is not good and does not care, or God is powerless to change the situation. The philosophical term for defending the justice of God in view of the reality of evil is *theodicy,* which comes from two Greek words, *theos* for God and *dike* for justice. A theodicy must respond to two forms of evil, natural evil and moral evil. Put simply—and therefore with some distortion—evil in nature is the price paid for the regularity of nature's laws. The same fuel that burns and powers a jet cannot suddenly stop burning if the jet crashes into a skyscraper. Moral evil represents the price for human freedom. The same hand that can reach out and comfort can strike and injure. For God to create a world that is ordered and not simply chaotic, there must be natural law. For there to be the possibility of good, ethical behavior—especially where we can love God and other human beings—there has to be freedom. This freedom allows for both good and evil action. This scope of this book does allow for an elaborate theodicy. I can simply sketch out the place of evil in God's drama with the cosmos from creation to eschatology, while emphasizing selected scientific discoveries that have affected our conceptions of evil and God's providence. Ultimately, all answers are tentative and cannot answer every objection. They work best when they leave some mystery to the way God has created the world and point to God's ultimate resolution in the crucifixion and the hope of consummation. (To pursue this topic further, see Kathryn J. Cameron's forthcoming book in this series, *Why Have You Forsaken Me?*)

The Bible takes evil as a given and resists extensive philosophical speculation. Instead it offers a distinctive realism and calls us to present practical, compassionate responses to evil. In Western societies, and particularly the United States, we have a general cultural allergy to admitting that evil is a daily reality. Still, we see evil not only in widespread calamities like earthquakes and war and personal suffering like cancer and injury, but also in daily spiritual-psychological brokenness. The Bible calls us to be healers in a world injured by evil and to become part of God's solution to evil. We mirror God's work through acts of compassion, and struggle to liberate people from evil. We respond through lament. We gain a foretaste of God's final victory over evil through prayer and worship. Evil raises considerable questions about the nature of God and God's creation, but it also offers concrete opportunities for doing God's work in the world.

No theodicy is complete without opening the "final chapter" of God's drama. There, at the end of history, God promises the end of evil. The book of Revelation reminds us of the biblical hope that, one day, God will remake the world and take away all evil and suffering. God's character and faithfulness secure this hope. At times this hope has been used by Christians to avoid engagement with the concrete problems of everyday life. It has been offered to the oppressed with no food now as "pie in the sky and the sweet by and by." This pseudo-solution distorts and manipulates the hope of heaven. The fulfillment of creation offers a vision for what life can be when we live fully consistent with God's will. Jesus himself taught the disciples to pray that God's "will be done, on earth as it is in heaven" (Matt. 6:10).

But there will be more on that in the next chapter. For now, we return to Darwin's earthquake and its theological aftershocks.

Darwin and the Fall

"Who came first, Adam or the dinosaurs?"

The third-grade Sunday school teacher is stumped as his student distills the problem Darwin laid at our feet. Neo-Darwinian evolution raises the question of whether Adam was a historical person or not. If Adam was not uniquely fashioned by the Creator's hand, what do we make of his "fall from grace"? There are two poles on the spectrum of Christian responses for relating the fall of Adam to the theory of evolution.

First of all, there is the approach of *the literal Adam:* Although many do not hold to this view, I want to make room for this perspective. It has an entirely respectable history. Many thoughtful Christians I know hold this view. I hope not to forfeit their goodwill if I, in the end, differ. Even with a commitment to evolutionary theory, one cannot discount the possibility that God specially created the literal Adam and Eve. In this view, Genesis 1 and 2 present a historical description of the first human beings. God specially created the first human beings, Adam and Eve. They initially lived in perfect relationship with God and their environment. By an abuse of free will—eating the fruit of the tree—they severed these relationships. Humankind lives under the curse of their sin but can be redeemed through the obedience of one "new Adam," Jesus Christ. Though even earlier commentators like Augustine and Origen represented alternative interpretations, this view more or less prevailed through the nineteenth century. It offers a relatively straightforward reading of Genesis 1–3, and makes sense of God's making creation originally "good," and then creation's falling to its current state. It also offers a space-time fall from grace, and the response of an actual space-time redemption in Jesus Christ.

It also has difficulties, including the fact that *adam* is simply a generic name for "the human being." The texts themselves slide between *adam* as a generic "human being" (Gen. 1:26; 4:25) and as "the *adam*" (1:27; 2:7–8, 15–16, 18–23, 25; 3:8–9, 12, 20, 22, 24). It is also hard for many to understand ethically that by this one man's sin, all subsequent human beings are born cursed to death and separation from God. It is difficult to reconcile with the macroevolution of human beings from earlier life forms. It is an uphill push against the weight of scientific evidence.

The other alternative might be called *the typological Adam.* Many today read Genesis as a representation of human existence, in which Adam represents a type of human being. Most Christians believe that to be thoughtful believers in an age of science means accepting macroevolution. Today's Homo sapiens evolved from earlier primates. In this view, Adam is a type or representative for our existence as human beings who struggle to use our freedom responsibly. In this view, hominid evolution involves the dawning of self- and God-consciousness. Polkinghorne summarizes this view:

> At some stage, the lure of self and the lure of the divine came into competition and there was a turning away from the pole of the divine Other and a turning into the pole of the human ego. Our ancestors became, in Luther's phrase, "curved in upon themselves." We are heirs of that culturally transmitted orientation. One does not need to suppose that this happened in a single decisive act; it would have been a stance that formed and reinforced itself through a succession of choices and actions. Death did not come into the world for the first time but rather mortality, the sad recognition of human finitude.[62]

Thus Adam's creation and fall are what we all face—a creation in God's image toward freedom as well as the pull to use that freedom destructively. Like Adam, we are glorious and horrible. And though we are currently in this state, the historical life and work of Jesus of Nazareth redeems us.

Although I affirm a commitment to creation by God over evolutionary science, I am not compelled to choose between the two. In fact, the doctrine of creation makes two primary affirmations: we are created in God's image, and the world is not fully consistent with God's intentions. With this in mind, there is ample room for scientific discovery. We also avoid dictating the best way for God to create. Instead we are to look concretely and openly at the evidence.

Overall, the Presbyterian Church has not seen a necessary conflict between evolution and the doctrine of creation, as I mentioned above. Similarly, the Roman Catholic Church has not felt compelled to decide between creation by God and evolution, although it argues that the soul is "immediately created" by God. And what is true for the Presbyterian Church (U.S.A.) and the Catholics can be extended to the U.S. populace. A 1999 Gallup poll found that 68 percent of American adults wanted to see both creationism and evolution in public schools. In addition, that same year, a People for the American Way Foundation poll found that the same percentage found no contradiction between evolution and the belief that God created us and guided human development.

Put simply, Christians believe God created us and our world. We can remain open as to how God accomplished it. I find no scientific argument that disproves God's creation. With that assertion in mind, I now turn to one possible counterargument: that genetic determinism proves neither we nor Adam have the ability to make free choices.

Genetic Determinism:
The Genes Made Me Do It!

God is free. We, as bearers of God's image, possess freedom. We as creatures are called to respond to God, to choose right over wrong. For that, we need freedom. At least that is our tradition. . . . But are really free? Determinism—the philosophy that everything we do has been programmed by forces beyond anyone's control— has supplied a recurring motif in the history of ideas. In the early nineteenth century, Pierre-Simon de Laplace stated baldly:

> An intelligence knowing, at a given instance of time, all forces acting in nature, as well as the momentary position of all things of which the universe consists, would be able to comprehend the motions of the largest bodies of the world and those of the lightest atoms in one single formula, provided his intellect were suf-

ficiently powerful to subject all data to analysis; to him nothing would be uncertain, both past and future would be present in his eyes?[63]

This suggests that everything, from a decision to marry to the outcome of the battle of Waterloo, has been fated.

Today determinism is back in a new form and tied with the revolutionary discoveries in genetics. The world-famous scientist Francis Crick, who codiscovered DNA, has laid down the gauntlet for those who defend the existence of human freedom. He comments on the title of his well-known book:

> The Astonishing Hypothesis is that "you," your joys and your sorrows, your memories and your ambitions, your sense of personal identity and free will, are in fact no more than the behavior of a vast assembly of nerve cells and their associated molecules. As Lewis Carroll's Alice might have phrased it: "You're nothing but a pack of neurons."[64]

If Crick is right, then we have some problems with our sense of freedom. In fact, it does not exist. And without freedom, we also have problems establishing ethics. The Christian tradition has located the ability to transcend our human, bodily limitations through the notion of the *soul*. The soul offers us freedom and the ability not just to be determined by our body. Unsurprisingly, Crick subtitled his book "The Scientific Search for the Soul." How then can we respond to Crick?

Of the many ways to refute his position—or most forms of determinism—the easiest is this: it is self-defeating. In a playful phrase, the biologist and theologian Arthur Peacocke has labeled the position "nothing buttery." (Remember Crick's rephrasing of Alice: "You're *nothing but* a pack of neurons.") Take Crick's argument to its conclusion. *If* our thinking processes are "nothing but" the interaction of biochemicals in the brain, then we have no way if what we know is true. It just is. We might as well call the size of our feet or the color of our hair "true." They are simply facts, neither right nor wrong. This makes Crick's wonderful discoveries "nothing but" the movement of electrical charges in his predetermined brain. But in fact, we know that some genetically influenced behavior patterns—a tendency toward violence or alcoholism—are not beneficial. Crick does not offer any means for assessing or responding to them.

Thankfully, we are not stuck with genetic determinism—or any determinism for that matter. Our faith has long taught that we are not just our bodies, but that our souls offer us transcendence from bodily processes, giving us freedom. Scientifically minded theologians talk about the soul as a capacity for transcendence and freedom rather than a "thing" that can be located through scientific experiments. In addition, Crick's arguments rest on *reductionism,* the notion that the workings of any system can be reduced to its smallest parts. But reductionism misses the point. Ted Peters, a theologian constantly exploring the effects of science on belief, has summarized it this way: "Determinism at the genetic level does not obviate free will at the person level. Genetic determinism just like all conditions of finitude places each person in his or her particular situation, readying the person to exercise freedom."[65] Our genetic makeup set the boundaries for our choices—not choices to "do anything" (as we often want freedom to mean). Our genetic structure is the chord structure over which we improvise our lives.

The Quantum Theology of Jazz

So as we have seen, evolutionary biology often is tied to determinism. On the other hand, contemporary physics, after the quantum revolution of 1900–1930, can hardly be considered deterministic. Perhaps evolutionary theory needs its own quantum revolution. In a deterministic model, the natural world is a closed box of cause and effect. This means that God must *intervene* to act in the natural world to answer prayers, to respond to cries for conversion, and to raise Jesus from the dead. In contrast, quantum theory implies that reality is open. Christian theology has also maintained that God continuously interacts with creation and therefore God does not have to intervene to act in the world. God is *always* interacting with nature. Integrating quantum theory and the Christian faith allows for a scientific means for a "noninterventionist" relationship between God and the world.

It all started in 1900, when the Berlin scientist Max Planck surprisingly discovered that light was not emitted in continuous waves (like water), but in packets, which he called "quanta" (the Latin word for "how much"). Thus the quantum revolution began. An essential element of this revolution is that there appears to be an irreducible quality of probability and flexibility at the most elemental level of nature. Werner Heisenberg's famous 1927 Uncertainty Principle encapsulates this key element in quantum reality: we can never know the exact position or momentum of quantum entities. Like focusing a camera, when we zero in on position, momentum fades, and vice versa. Put another way, there is no exact position or momentum until quantum entities are observed.

Heisenberg, later formulating these ideas philosophically in his 1955–1956 contribution to the famed Gifford Lectures, reinvigorated the notion of *potentia* from Aristotelian philosophy ("potentiality" or "possibility").[66] In other words, these entities only have a *potential* state until they are observed. At the subatomic level, the world exhibits an incompleteness and limitation, characteristics that require God's activity. After reviewing the significance of quantum theory for our understanding of nature, Robert Russell, the head of Berkeley's world-renowned Center for Theology and the Natural Sciences, offers this conclusion:

> In short, and metaphorically, what one could say is that what we normally take as "nature" is in reality the activity of "God + nature." Alternatively, from this perspective we really do not know what the world would be like *without* God's action.[67]

God truly interacts with and sustains the created world, and yet the world has freedom. Too often the understanding of God's plan and providence have become frozen in some sort of "absolute decree," an unchanging plan that has no place for improvisation. (I once read in the humor magazine *The Door* that this is the World Wrestling Federation view of reality in which the outcome is predetermined!) Nature certainly has fixity. Thoughtful scientists and theologians all remind us that nature is consistent and its processes are open to explanation. Indeed regularity allows for free action. The Lord also speaks of the surprise in continually creating what has never been before. "Behold, I am doing a new thing; now it springs up, do you not perceive it? I will make a way in the wilderness and rivers in the desert" (Isa. 43:19).

When God becomes incarnate in Jesus Christ—the crucial place for understanding Christian theology and therefore its dialogue with science—there is not just a fixed plan, but also room for a responsive interchange. In one of the most stunning passages in the Gospels, Jesus encounters a Syrophoenician woman (Mark 7:24–30), whom he is tempted to pass by, saying that he is sent to feed the "children of Israel." She calls him back to serve her, and he responds by healing her daughter of a demon.

How then can we picture the dynamic relationship between the God of Jesus Christ and the world? Early in the twentieth century, the philosopher William James offered the idea of God as the Grand Master of cosmic chess, always responding to and never baffled by the moves of the creaturely opponent and sure to have the final checkmate.[68]

As rich as this metaphor is, the world is not just an opponent to God. God's interaction with the world involves play and creativity. As an alternative image, I propose that we, God and the world, play together in a cosmic jazz improvisation. "Improv," the essence of jazz music, signifies the spontaneous and unique molding of musical form. Miles Davis could solo on *Kind of Blue* a thousand times, and it was never exactly the same. Similarly, the jazz pianist and Presbyterian pastor Bill Carter speaks of composition (what has been written or "decreed") and performance (what happens in the moment) fusing in improvisation. God's plan and laws of nature fuse in an ongoing interaction with creatures to form something truly creative. The structure and plan are already in place—there is no chaos—so God can still achieve particular ends. It is not, however, altogether fixed.

In jazz, there are three critical components: knowing your instrument, having a firm grasp of the music (especially the chord changes), and really listening to your other musicians. A common misconception is that jazz improvisation is simply "playing what feels good." But it is the preparation and competence—Miles's knowledge of his horn—that allow for spontaneity. In terms of creation, God's power and preparation are so sure that God does not have to work with automata. The Master Improviser's creativity is so deep that the Lord can take the components of what the created order contributes, and then freely improvise with them. God can even take our bad notes and form something beautiful and good.

The Persistence of Care:
The Doctrine of Providence

Some of us, when we were kids, memorized the 1563 Heidelberg Catechism. It confesses—really almost proclaims—that God did not just wind the watch and let it keep ticking.

Q: What do you understand by the providence of God?

A: The almighty and ever-present power of God whereby he still upholds, as it were by his own hand, heaven and earth together with all creatures, and rules in such a way that leaves and grass, rain and drought, fruitful and unfruitful years, food and drink, health and sickness, riches and poverty, and everything else, come to us not by chance but by his fatherly hand.

These are comforting words that stand at the heart of the Christian faith. I know more than one crisis where they have strengthened me and others. Still, the reality of life forces "and yet" upon the catechism's answer. And yet . . . those same people who make this stirring affirmation have also held a dying father in our arms. And yet . . . others have heard those three cruel words: "You have cancer." And yet . . . almost all have watched scenes of terrorism broadcast over satellite TV or dispersed through the Internet. Each of these presents a case against the goodness of creation. The comfort and assurance of God's presence can fade. Evil hits us every day like a prosecuting attorney, cross-examining nature as God's witness, arguing a case against God's care for the world.

Here the doctrine of providence comes to the test. So it is important to understand what the term means. The word derives from two Latin roots (*pro-videre*) that mean to "fore-see," which also includes the concept of looking ahead so as to "provide."

Webster's definition is rather concise: "divine guidance or care." From this foundation, Christian theologians have sorted out three related components to providence (if you read again the question from the Heidelberg Catechism you will find each of them):

- *Preservation:* God sustains all creatures in their distinctive natures and powers.
- *Cooperation:* God not only sustains but actively concurs in these creatures' action in such an intimate way that every action of these beings can be ultimately explained only by reference to both their and God's actions.
- *Government:* God fulfills the purpose of all creatures by guiding them.

The Drew Seminary theologian Thomas Oden, who has worked tirelessly and effectively to rejuvenate classical insights, summarizes providence this way: "Three affirmations summarize the Christian teaching of providence: God is preserving the creation in being. God is cooperating to enable creatures to act. God is guiding all creatures, inorganic and organic, animal and rational creation, toward a purposeful end that exceeds the understanding of those being provided for."[69]

So what is the bottom line? *God continues to interact with creation.*

If I were to choose the basic biblical text on providence, it is that sometimes misapplied passage from Romans 8:28: "We know that God works for the good in all things to those who love God and who have been called according to his purpose" (my translation). The eminent English pastor and biblical scholar John Stott lists "five unshakable convictions" from this text.[70] He first points out that what "we know" contrasts to v. 26, where Paul admits that "we do not know how to pray as we ought."

1. *God works:* Even when we do not see it—or believe it— God's action on our behalf is constant. This is the essence of faith and the central conviction of providence.
2. *for the good* of the people of God: All things are done for our benefit. This affirmation does not mean that every single event is good!

3. *in all things*: In our lives, in the natural world, and even in suffering (v. 17 says that we "suffer with God" and that we have "groanings" with all creation in vv. 23 and 24).

4. *to those who love God*: This is not a general statement, but one directed toward believers—and one should add not focused on individuals, but on the family of God as a whole.

5. *who have been called according to his purpose*: the key factor in determining "the good" is that it is ultimately for God's plan.

Even after these affirmations, Stott is quick to add, "These are five truths about God which, Paul writes, *we know*. We do not always understand what God is doing, let alone welcome it. Nor are we told that he is at work for our comfort. But we know that in all things he is working towards our supreme good."[71]

We must never deny evil because of our belief in God's providence. Evil experiences are really evil. God, however, can work through them to make good. Ultimately this is a statement about God's power, creativity, and goodness. God can improvise over bad notes to create a beautiful song. Therefore, Christians can echo Jeremiah's declaration to the Israelite exiles: " 'I know the plans I have for you,' declares the Lord, 'plans to prosper you and not to harm you, plans to give you hope and a future' " (Jer. 29:11).

The Other Side of Love:
Living with Grace in a Hurting World

So, if providence is meant to comfort us, what do we do in the face of a job loss, a cancer diagnosis, or a friend's betrayal? The central Christian virtue of love takes on a new meaning in light of evil and sin. Certainly, it takes the form of the cross. On the one hand (the vertical dimension), we receive God's care and are assured of divine providence. On the other (horizontal), we offer grace to others.

One consistent theme I have faced as a pastor is how to make it when the going gets tough. How can we be assured that God's working when we cannot see it? George Hunsinger, a contemporary

Protestant theologian attuned to real-life concerns, offers these words on providence: "When I am beset by bitterness or despair, I can withstand them by heeding five biblical principles of spiritual counsel."[72] He continues:

1. Receive everything as from the hand of God. God is in control. "Are not two sparrows sold for a penny? Yet not one of them will fall to the ground apart from your Father" (Matt. 10:29).
2. Keep your focus on the Lord. When I shift my focus to other factors, all seems lost. "But when [Peter] noticed the strong wind, he became frightened, and beginning to sink, he cried out, 'Lord, save me!'" (Matt. 14:30).
3. Cling to the promises of God. Immerse yourself in Scripture and use it to call on God in prayer. (See Matt. 14:30 above.)
4. Seek wise counselors. God does not ask us to bear our burdens alone. "Bear one another's burdens, and in this way you will fulfill the law of Christ" (Gal. 6:2).
5. Expect new life. God will not fail to turn my affliction into good. "But those who wait for the LORD shall renew their strength, they shall mount up with wings like eagles, they shall run and not be weary, they shall walk and not faint" (Isa. 40:31).

Evil hits us not only from outside, but also from the inside. We cause evil toward others. Forgiveness represents the critical act of Christian love. The logic remains simple and persuasive. Because God has forgiven our sins in Christ, we are compelled and freed to forgive others. Pain and resentment ultimately, when not forgiven, kill us. Prayers of confession help us bring to God our hurts, and there God heals us. Conversation—and real truth-telling—bring to light what has been hidden. The sacraments especially signify the essence of this form of love. The first step of the Christian life, baptism, acknowledges that we all start from a common point, our need. "The ground is level at the foot of the cross"—and at the baptismal font. We all start by recognizing our equality of brokenness. Then, in Communion, we realize again our common call to turn around from enmity and turn toward one another in love. Jesus is very clear when he sets this in terms of worship generally:

If you enter your place of worship and, about to make an offering, you suddenly remember a grudge a friend has against you, abandon your offering, leave immediately, go to this friend and make things right. Then and only then, come back and work things out with God. (Matt. 5:23–24, *The Message*[73])

The basic idea is that, if we want nearness to God, we need to seek it with our sisters and brothers in the faith. (Our four basic relationships are interrelated.)

To live in light of evil and suffering is to reach the profound limitation of words. More than talk and insight, the smallest touch of grace lifts the heaviest burden. As Job discovered, God remains the ultimate answer. "When pain is borne, a little courage helps more than much knowledge, a little human sympathy more than much courage, and the least tincture of the love of God more than all" (C. S. Lewis).[74]

5

God's Not Finished with Us Yet:
The New Creation (or Eschatology)

For this reason [the saints] are before the throne of God,
    and worship him day and night within his temple,
    and the one who is seated on the throne will shelter
        them.
They will hunger no more, and thirst no more;
    the sun will not strike them,
    nor any scorching heat;
    for the Lamb at the center of the throne will be their
        shepherd,
    and he will guide them to springs of the water of life,
and God will wipe away every tear from their eyes.

Revelation 7:15–17

Death, be not proud, though some have callèd thee
    Mighty and dreadful, for thou art not so:
For those whom thou think'st thou dost overthrow
    Die not, poor Death; nor yet canst thou kill me.
    From Rest and Sleep, which but thy picture be,
Much pleasure, then from thee much more must flow;
    And soonest our best men with thee do go—
        Rest of their bones and souls' delivery!
Thou'rt slave to fate, chance, kings, and desperate men,
    And dost with poison, war, and sickness dwell;
        And poppy or charms can make us sleep as well
    And better than thy stroke. Why swell'st thou then?
        One short sleep past, we wake eternally,
    And Death shall be no more; Death, thou shalt die!

John Donne

*E*very year, I consider it one of life's greatest aesthetic pleasures to listen to George Frideric Handel's Messiah. Our Easter worship service at Fifth Avenue Presbyterian always ends with the stirring words of the "Hallelujah!" chorus. The trumpet blends with triumphant organ and voices. Our doors swing open, and a crowd gathers on Fifth Avenue, listening curiously to the stirring words of John's Revelation set to the exultant music of Handel.

> Hallelujah, for the Lord God Omnipotent reigneth, Hallelujah!
>
> (Rev. 19:6)

> The Kingdom of this world is become the Kingdom of our Lord, and of His Christ; and He shall reign for ever and ever, Hallelujah!
>
> (Rev. 11:15)

> King of Kings, and Lord of Lords, and He shall reign for ever and ever, Hallelujah!
>
> (Rev. 19:16)

Without any overstatement, this brings worship into the absolute proper place—a "preview of coming attractions," a step into the realm of heaven, hearing the songs that the angels sing. It brings us to Jesus Christ, who offers salvation and who reigns as Lord of Lords in heaven.

This same Jesus Christ we meet in our earthly life in worship, the sacraments, and prayer is the One we meet at the end of time. Christians have no reason to fear him and every reason for hope. As we reach the final chapter (both of this book and of God's story), I am reminded of this comforting affirmation. The mystery—and fear—of the future can only be assuaged by God's promise of life in Jesus Christ. Whether we dread our own death or the destruction of the universe, there is one response: Jesus Christ. Jesus Christ answers with the promise of the new creation.

How else can we respond to Macbeth's bitter denunciation of every human life?

> I am sick at heart. . . .
> . . . .
> To-morrow, and to-morrow, and to-morrow,
> Creeps in this petty pace from day to day,
> To the last syllable of recorded time;
> . . . .
> Life's but a walking shadow, a poor player
> That struts and frets his hour upon the stage,
> And then is heard no more; it is a tale
> Told by an idiot, full of sound and fury,
> Signifying nothing.
>
> (*Macbeth* 5.3.24, 5.5)

The sheer futility of life, always circumscribed by death, could push us to conclude that our existence is a tragedy. "A useless passion," the French existentialist Jean-Paul Sartre once bitterly scoffed. Macbeth and Sartre have a point. Life is a futile tragedy where the imprint of good is washed over by the waves of time and death and decay.

But thankfully we do not live simply within the confines of earthly life. Jesus' resurrection and promise of new creation offers a rejoinder to the tragic futility of life, whether that be life of an individual or of the cosmos. This makes for joy and laughter because the ending is good. Instead of a tragedy, we are in a comedy. Theologians call that final act of triumph in the dramatic comedy *eschatology.*

Eschatology comes from two Greek words, *eschatos,* which means "final" or "last," and *logos,* which means "discussion" or "study of." Together eschatology signifies the discussion or study of the last things. The "end times" represents another contemporary phrase. A related term, "apocalypse," means literally "unveiling" or "revelation." It signifies the final unveiling of God's plan for the world and often includes the final battle between good and evil, preceded by signs. Similarly, apocalyptic literature—like the biblical book of Revelation—portrays the end of the world and of human history as a great struggle between the forces of God and of Satan, with God the victor.

And yet, we are mistaken to think of eschatology as something

only in the future, because Jesus' resurrection initiates the fulfillment of all things. We live "between the times"—between Christ's
first coming and resurrection and Christ's second coming. Certainly, eschatology includes such august topics as Christ's second
coming, the resurrection of the dead, the final judgment, heaven
and hell. We must also include the Christian life lived under the
promise of new creation.

For Christian believers, these topics burst with hope. But the
dogs of despair constantly nip at our heels. They bark the despon-
dency of a culture increasingly cynical about eternal life and the
hope of God's future for creation. Consider the example of Mel
Blanc, who provided the famous voices of Porky Pig, Bugs Bunny,
and most of the Warner Brothers' Looney Tunes characters. When
he died a few years ago, Porky Pig's closing line was chiseled in
Blanc's tombstone: "That's all folks!" And that exclamation poses
the questions we face. Is death the final chapter of our lives? Is the
destruction of the universe the ultimate purpose of God's creation?
Jesus Christ, the great Yes from the God of Life, replies with a
decisive No.

Still, the fact of death terrifies and motivates us. As Benjamin
Franklin quipped, only death and taxes are certain. In *The Denial
of Death,* psychologist Ernest Becker argued that the fear of death
"haunts the human animal like nothing else; it is a mainspring of
human activity—activity designed largely to avoid the fatality of
death, to overcome it by denying in some way that it is the final
destiny for man."[75] Sometimes our denial takes the form of a
straightforward quest for earthly immortality. A friend's sister
moved to Arizona to join a cult that awaits the day when proper
thinking and diet make us live forever—not in some other realm,
but here on earth. This is not new. In 1513 Ponce de Leon set out
in search of the elusive "fountain of youth." He had heard that this
mythical spring produced the waters of everlasting life, a secular
alternative to the "rivers of living water" that Jesus promised in
John 7:38. And just up the street from my office on Fifth Avenue,
the Metropolitan Museum of Art displays an extensive, historic
campaign to deny death. There lie the splendid remains of the
Egyptian pharaohs with their elaborate schemes about personal

immortality, whose glorious pyramids and ornate sarcophagi describe in exacting detail the nature of life after death.

We seek eternal life. It is in our bones. The skeptic dismisses this yearning as vain hope, as the childlike speculation of an infantile era. But as children we learn many things. When we sense danger, we need protection. When we are tired, we require sleep. When we are hungry, we need to eat. Our hunger for everlasting life is a natural appetite created for God by God. Death is unnatural to us. For centuries our culture has increasingly tried to suppress a yearning for heaven, and yet the desire continues. And our environment must be mistaken. Our yearning for heaven is a sign in us of God's promise of everlasting life.

Apocalypse Soon?
The Millennium Has Turned

But eschatology does not merely concern individual eternal life. Its scope is the entire created order. The year 2000 sparked renewed speculation about the "end times" and the destruction of the entire cosmos. In the vestiges of our society's cultural Christianity lurks the memory of the thousand years of Christ. Revelation 20:4 speaks of a day when the saints "came to life and reigned with Christ a thousand years." Okay, maybe we will remember it as the *two thousand* year reign. At any rate, a multiple of 1,000 seems a good number for the end of the world. This furor became heightened by the "Y2K" scare—that computer failure caused by the need for an extra digit in silicon memory would cause computers to break down. Massive disruption of basic services would follow. No one would be able to attain water, heat, or food. Riots would erupt. Bill Clinton would call a state of emergency and become the effective dictator of the United States. Are such dire times the "wars and rumors of war," the "birth-pangs" (Matt. 24:8) that Jesus predicted before he comes again? Of course, this sounds absurd now: Americans awoke on January 1, 2000, with laptops working, water running from the tap, heat pouring out, and president in the White House, but not on a throne.

With Y2K almost a distant memory, it might now be easier to notice that the third millennium after Jesus' birth probably began around 1996 or 1997. Why? A Greek monk named Dionysius Exiguus in Rome was commissioned in 532 A.D. to develop a new, Gregorian calendar. Based on the existing Roman calendar, he worked to begin with Jesus' birth at year 1, *anno domini* ("the year of the Lord"). Unfortunately, Jesus was born while Herod was alive (see Matt. 2:1). Using Exiguus's calendar, Herod died in spring 4 B.C. Thus Jesus was born before his own birthdate (or something like that).

But end times speculation cannot be confined to the year 2000. Over the last twenty years, I personally experienced several apocalyptic predictions. Even before I had formed theological antennae, the California pastor Hal Lindsey had created a national furor in the 1970s with his bestseller *The Late, Great Planet Earth*. In 1988, on our cross-country drive to Princeton for seminary, my wife and I stopped in MacPherson, Kansas. That Sunday we attended a church service, where the pastor and greeters distributed a booklet called "88 Reasons Why the Rapture Will Happen in 1988." My favorite assertion of a long list? That Christ "doesn't know the day or hour" (Matt. 24:36) *because of time zones*. In other words, for him to say "6:15 P.M." would only work for 1/24 of the planet. Even before my New Testament classes at Princeton, I found that interpretation suspect.

Then, only six years later, I received a call from New College, Berkeley. CNN had contacted this school of theology to request a commentator on a current end times scenario. And so in just two hours, unprepared and therefore dressed in shorts and a cotton sweater, I found myself on camera, interviewed by a rather congenial Craig Heaps about the engineer and radio commentator, Harold Camping. From Camping's Oakland "Family Radio" ministry headquarters, he predicted the strong possibility of the second coming of Christ in 1994. (I was at least heartened by Camping's realization that our Gregorian calendar had a serious flaw. He believed that Jesus was born in 6 B.C.) Heaps asked me, "What do you think is the danger of this type of speculation?" My answer: that it would distract us from the task of preaching of gospel and bringing about the kingdom of God on earth. And that remains my concern.

If it is not speculation on the date of Christ's return, we constantly press toward filling in other details. Even today, despite increasing skepticism about the truth of the Bible, Americans seem still hungry to know specifics about the last days. Consider the Tim LaHaye and Jerry B. Jenkins's novel *The Indwelling,* one of the Left Behind series on the events of the apocalypse. In the summer of 2000, it rose to the unprecedented height for Christian fiction as the *New York Times* number-one fiction bestseller. As a cultural index, it reveals that we want particulars. In a time that seems to be out of control, we crave assurance and specific answers about the way that God controls the future. We can name the scourge: drug abuse, Newt Gingrich, Hillary Clinton, lies from the media, AIDS, guns in schools. Whatever evil we name, it seems rampant and pervasive, and we yearn for good to triumph.

Both God's control and the ultimate victory of good represent worthy concerns. The problem is, we grasp for a map instead of the Guide. We demand answers from God instead of a relationship with God. Oswald Chambers, author of the still popular *My Utmost for His Highest,* has put the issue succinctly: "It is spiritual lust to seek answers from God instead of seeking God, who is our answer." Christ and the biblical writers offer enough to nurture our faith and provide assurance, but not enough to satisfy our every speculation. Jesus often spoke in symbols about the end, and distinctly denied knowing the exact day. Let us make sure not to seek to know more than Christ about his second coming.

My focus rests first on Jesus Christ. He remains the ultimate answer to the question of the world's destiny. "We don't know what the future holds, but we know who holds the future." Only God has the exhaustive answers for our eternal life and for the destiny of the cosmos. Secondarily, through the biblical witness, we see important contours of the future, but not a detailed map. It is not exhaustive, but sufficient. Before surveying the biblical material, it is fascinating to look at the relation between theological and scientific understandings of the end.

The Science of the End

John Polkinghorne, the particle physicist and theologian, spoke to his assembled, attentive audience for the University of Edinburgh's Gifford Lectures in 1993–1994. He reminded them that cosmologists do not only peer into the past. They also attempt to discern the future. On a cosmic scale, he noted, science tells the story of the end of the universe. Its history is an enormous tug-of-war between the expansive force of the Big Bang, driving the galaxies apart, and the contractive force of gravity, pulling them together. If expansion continues, the galaxies will continue to separate, and the universe will decay into low-grade radiation. Continued contraction will collapse the universe into a fiery, big crunch. These two effects are so evenly balanced that we cannot tell which will win.[76]

William Stoeger, a world-class astronomer and staff scientist for the Vatican Observatory, has added a few possibilities for our earth's demise in an article with the daunting title "Scientific Accounts of Ultimate Catastrophes in Our Life-Bearing Universe." They are these: destruction of earth by asteroids and comets, the decline of our sun, and the explosion of a nearby supernova.[77] However it arrives, the destruction of life on earth remains certain.

But we come then to a significant problem for Christian faith. These endings hardly represent the glorious fulfillment of "a new heaven and a new earth" that Revelation 21:1 promises. But Polkinghorne reminded his listeners in Edinburgh that "Cosmic death and human death pose equivalent questions of what is God's intention for his creation."[78] Only God offers hope. God's new creation will be a transformation of the current order, no less surprising than our resurrection, initiated by Jesus' resurrection at the first Easter.

How can Christians relate scientific cosmology and Christian eschatology? There is a comparable scientific phenomenon to God's continual work in the world. Evolutionary science depicts the created order as constantly unfolding into ever greater complexity. Quantum theory's indeterminacy describes creation as irreducibly open ended. I am reminded again of a jazz chart—the basic melody and chord structure are written out, but the actual song has elements of surprise or improvisation. The future depicted by scientific cosmology displays openness to creating "new things" (as in Isa. 43:19) and thus to God's continual action in the world.

On the other hand, science does not provide complete answers to the end of the world. It offers an ending only in the sense of how the physical system will probably run down. It does not, indeed cannot, speak of the end in the sense of a goal or direction. Science cannot—if it remains true to its own parameters—speak of forces outside of nature. Even with science in hand, theologians come to the question of whether Christ's return relates directly to the destruction of the universe as a whole or specifically of the earth, or whether the end of this world is simply an act of God without natural precedent. Put bluntly, will Jesus return because an asteroid destroys the earth?

Regarding God's action, science must therefore remain silent. At best, scientific study may lead us to the threshold, but cannot open the door to God. Here we come to the limit of general revelation, of God's disclosure through nature. Only in God's revelation in Scripture can we find the new creation.

The Resurrection of Christ

Science describes only indirectly ways the world may end. The Bible, however, speaks clearly of God's directing the final act of the cosmic drama. Three times Revelation (1:8, 21:6, 22:13) calls the Lord the "Alpha and Omega," which represent the first and last letters of the Greek alphabet. Nothing precedes nor slips away from God. God knows the entire history of creation. We can discern the script of this history through Scripture of both old and new creation.

The initiating act of the new creation is the resurrection of Jesus Christ on the first Easter, the third day after his death on a cross. And there, at the cross of Christ, one must begin. There we find the most heavily attested historical fact of Jesus' life. Two historians, the Roman Tacitus in about 110 A.D. and the first-century Jewish chronicler Josephus, clearly speak of Christ's death on a cross. Besides, the disciples had no reason to make it up. The cross represented a shameful, four-letter word in Latin, *crux,* since it signified a death reserved for political traitors and villains and never for Roman citizens. Cicero's *Orations* denounced both the reality of the cross and its usage by polite Romans. Death on a cross was "the most cruel and abominable form of punishment," and the very word "should be foreign not only to the body of a Roman citizen, but to his thoughts, his eyes, his ears."[79]

Here the science of medicine also has something to say. A physician can describe death as painful, as excruciating (from the Latin *excruciatus,* "out of the cross"). Death by crucifixion damaged no vital organs. The crucified sufferers could no longer lift themselves, and the weight of their bodies rested on their chest and did not allow them to breathe. Death usually came slowly through dehydration or asphyxiation.

Out of this shame and surprise—for no Jew could conceive that the messiah would ever have died this death—a surprising testimony arose: "Christ died for our sins in accordance with the scriptures, and that he was buried, and that he was raised on the third day in accordance with the scriptures." Paul wrote this earliest written record around 55 A.D. in the First Letter to the Corinthians (chap. 15), saying that 500 others witnessed this appearance. In these appearances, Jesus' resurrected body at times resembles ours, such as when he urges Thomas to touch his wounds (John 20:27). He also appears unlike a normal body when he disappears suddenly (Luke 24:31). This new creation is both similar to and dissimilar from the old creation. To the degree that one finds correspondence to this world, science can offer insight. To the degree it speaks of a new creation, science has little to add.

The resurrection of Christ restored the disciples' faith and hope and sent them on a mission. It also vindicated Jesus as Messiah, turning the shame of the cross into God's victory over death and sin. Finally, the resurrection of Christ initiates the new creation. On that first Easter morning, as Jesus cracked open the tomb and burst forth, the crack of the new creation spread through the old creation and has not stopped since.

The Second Coming of Christ

Few have offered a more gripping introduction to the theme of the second coming than the poet W. B. Yeats (no friend to orthodox Christianity) in his 1921 poem of the same name:

> Turning and turning in the widening gyre
> The falcon cannot hear the falconer;
> Things fall apart; the centre cannot hold;
> Mere anarchy is loosed upon the world,
> The blood-dimmed tide is loosed, and everywhere
> The ceremony of innocence is drowned;
> The best lack all conviction, while the worst
> Are full of passionate intensity.
>
> Surely some revelation is at hand;
> Surely the Second Coming is at hand.

The Bible offers language no less world-ending, world-transforming, and world-beginning. It first foretells and then promises Christ's second coming. The Hebrew Scriptures provide the backdrop for his return. Jesus employed a key Old Testament concept, the Son of Man (here the traditional and literal rendering of *ben adam*) to describe the event of his return. In the book of Daniel, the setting is Israel's captivity under the oppressive thumb of Babylon following the destruction of the prized city of Jerusalem in 586 B.C. Daniel has visions of four kingdoms—Babylonian, Median, Persian, Greek—represented by a lion, a bear, a four-headed winged leopard, and a ten-horned dragon-like beast. Then comes the establishment of a fifth, eternal kingdom. Jewish tradition interprets this final kingdom as the Messiah's. (By the way, "Messiah" and "Christ" represent the same meaning in Hebrew and Greek respectively. Both mean literally "the anointed.") Christian biblical scholars, with an eye toward God's coming as a human being in Christ, highlight that animals symbolized the previous kingdoms and that here the kingdom comes in a *human* form as the Son of Man.

> As I watched in the night visions,
> I saw one like the Son of Man

> coming with the clouds of heaven.
> And he came to the Ancient One
>   and was presented before him.
> To him was given dominion
>   and glory and kingship,
> That all peoples, nations, and languages
>   should serve him.
> His dominion is an everlasting dominion
>   that shall not pass away,
> and his kingship is one
>   that shall never be destroyed.
> (Dan. 7:13–14, translation
altered for clarity)

Jesus reshapes this figure of the Son of Man and thus refashions expectations for the Messiah (a crucial sticking point in Jewish-Christian dialogue). Instead of one advent as a politically dominant liberator, the Messiah appears twice. He comes in the meekness of a baby and returns as the righteous and powerful Savior and Judge. The first time arrives with the opportunity to turn our lives around, "Repent, and believe in the good news!" (Mark 1:15). At the second time, the opportunity for repentance has passed. In Matthew 24 (told in parallel in Mark 13 and Luke 21), Jesus looks toward the end of history. He foresees that signs and particularly suffering will proceed the end when the Son of Man will appear to gather the elect.

> Immediately after the suffering of those days
>   the sun will be darkened,
>   and the moon will not give its light;
>   the stars will fall from heaven,
>   and the powers of heaven will be shaken.

Then the sign of the Son of Man will appear in heaven, and then all the tribes of the earth will mourn, and they will see the "Son of Man coming on the clouds of heaven" with power and great glory. And he will send out his angels with a loud trumpet call, and they will gather his elect from the four winds, from one end of heaven to the other.

(Matt. 24:29–31)

But Jesus quickly adds, "But about that day and hour no one knows, neither the angels of heaven nor the Son, but only the Father" (24:36).

In Matthew 25, Jesus follows this prediction with three parables. One concerns ten bridesmaids, only half of whom prepared for the customary arrival of the bridegroom. The second describes three recipients of various amounts of money or "talents," a huge sum in the first century. The boss gives them five million dollars, two and half million, and half a million (in today's terms). He then encourages them to invest. Finally, a shepherd separates the righteous "sheep" from the unrighteous "goats" based on their good deeds toward society's outcasts. Though each has its unique features, the similarities speak most clearly. All depict a separation of two types of response—bold investing vs. fearful inactivity, attentive preparation vs. lazy indolence, unself-conscious compassion vs. inattentive hard-heartedness. Each parable encourages action in light of a cataclysmic moment. All describe some period of delay during which we wait and work. All three parables remind us to be ready and awake.[80] (A single Greek word, *gregoreo,* stands behind this combination, and since it represents the root of my first name, I could not pass up the opportunity to mention it.)

Jesus does not command an emotion, but a healthy expectation that transforms everything we do. C. S. Lewis explains it this way:

> We cannot always be excited. We can, perhaps, train ourselves to ask more and more often how the thing which we are saying or doing (or failing to do) at each moment will look when the irresistible light streams in upon it; that light which is so different from the light of this world—and yet, even now, we know just enough of it to take it into account.[81]

This call to be *gregoreo* encourages neither unreasonable excitement nor fearful paralysis. Instead it calls us to act today because we live under the promise of fulfillment. The parables all lead to greater rewards: attending a joyous wedding, receiving more money, "entering into the joy of your master."

I imagine an analogy. I have seen many promising artists wait for their break in New York City. You are a starving young jazz pianist. Every day you practice, hoping to be discovered. Most of your hours are filled with waiting tables in order to pay the bills so that you can audition. And even after years of hard work, nothing's happening. On a random Tuesday morning, you are in a church sanctuary, working through your standard practice regime, engaging your gift and passion for the piano. Unceremoniously, a stranger walks in. He listens attentively, but without interruption. When you are finished, you are greeted with applause and these words: "Hi, I'm Wynton Marsalis, and I need a pianist for the Lincoln Center Jazz Orchestra. Are you free?"

The Resurrection of the Body

A few years back, in the heyday of *Saturday Night Live,* I saw a skit in which a couple of cynical, chatty, flip, urbane New Yorkers interviewed contemporary personalities. In one segment, these interviewers questioned the guy who displays "John 3:16" at football games as a witness to the gospel. Why does he do it? He responded clearly, "So that others may believe in Jesus Christ and have eternal life." After this stark reply, one interviewer queried the other:

> "Do you believe we'll live forever?"
> "I hope not in this body!"

They both exploded in catty laughter, either masking deeper anxiety or revealing a shocking shallowness. In any event, that was the end of the conversation! A topic like everlasting life treated with such mocking! The problem for them was—with sagging jaw lines and increasing flab—do we really want this body to take us into eternity? Obviously they misread the intention of eternal life. The Christian church does not teach that we will live forever in this earthly body. What then do the Christians mean by the doctrine of the resurrection of the body?

The apostle Paul concerns himself throughout his writings with the persistent question of suffering (a form of theodicy). Why must God's people suffer when we are following God's will for us in Jesus Christ? Romans 8:18–25 provides the most extensive responses. He begins by expanding the scope to the entire creation, "the universe" in contemporary terms. (Paul uses *creation* three times in vv. 19, 20, and 21.) The people of God groan, with all non-human creation, because our destinies have been wrapped together. But suffering does not have the final word. A cry arises in us as a sign of something more. We *hope* for glory. For Paul, our hope does not represent vain presumption, but secure expectation. That long-expected, glorious day will also dry all tears.

What does Paul say specifically about the new creation? He affirms that there will be *glory* (vv. 18 and 21)—a word for the divine presence in fullness, in this case unveiled in Christ's final coming. Paul looks to *freedom* (v. 21) from decay—that the fallenness of the world will cease. And so we look forward with *hope* (vv. 24–25), which is the theological virtue that corresponds to God's future, to the final triumph of the cosmic comedy. Finally, God's *Spirit* represents the *first payment* of this new creation (v. 23)—there will be the fullness of joy that we now only know in part.

Paul contemplates the resurrection of the body most extensively in 1 Corinthians 15:35–44. Paul, as many after him, struggles with an apt analogy for resurrection. His conclusion offers profound hope. Eugene Peterson's fresh contemporary paraphrase, *The Message,* gives it directness:

> Some skeptic is sure to ask, "Show me how resurrection works. Give me a diagram; draw me a picture. What does this 'resurrection body' look like?" If you look at this question closely, you'll realize how absurd it is. There are no diagrams for this kind of thing. We do have a parallel experience in gardening. You plant a "dead" seed; soon there is a flourishing plant. There is no visual likeness between seed and plant. You could never guess what a tomato would look like by looking at a tomato seed. What we plant in the soil and what grows out of it don't look anything alike. The dead body that we bury in the ground and the resurrection body that comes from it will be dramatically different.
>
> You will notice that the variety of bodies is stunning. Just as there are different kinds of seeds, there are different kinds of

bodies—humans, animals, birds, fish—each unprecedented in
its form. You get a hint at the diversity of resurrection glory by
looking at the diversity of bodies not only on earth but in the
skies—sun, moon, stars—all varieties of beauty and brightness.
And we're looking at pre-resurrection "seeds"—who can imagine what the resurrection "plants" will be like!

This image of planting a dead seed and raising a live plant
is a mere sketch at best, but perhaps it will help in approaching
the mystery of the resurrection body—but only if you keep in
mind that when we're raised, we're raised for *good,* alive forever! The corpse that's planted is no beauty, but when it's
raised, it's glorious. Put in the ground weak, it comes up powerful. The seed sown is natural; the seed grown is supernatural—same seed, same body, but what a difference from when
it goes down in physical mortality to when it is raised up in
spiritual immortality!

Certainly, every detail about our resurrection is not fully laid out.
Paul is trying to understand and express the depths of the God. At
several other places—in 1 Corinthians 2:9–10, for example—he
simply admits the limits of his understanding:

But, as it is written, "What no eye has seen, nor ear heard,
Nor human heart conceived,
What God has prepared for those who love him"—
These things God has revealed to us through the Spirit;
    for the Spirit searches everything, even the depths of God.

Overall, Paul sketches these great promises, but leaves the details
open.

But as a pastor, I know that church members remain unsatisfied
with only generalities. In fact, when I have taught this material in
adult education classes, the specifics captivate the students. Once
I presented the idea that the immortality of the soul was not a truly
Christian teaching, but a loan from Plato who taught that the body
was mortal and decaying and the soul inherently immortal. Once
we died, Plato asserted, we thankfully freed ourselves from the
shackles of the body. I countered (as presented in chapter three)
that Hebrew thought conceives of human beings as a unity of body

and soul. The class was not pleased to hear this denial of our soul's immortality. They did not want to taste death. (It reminded me of Woody Allen's quip, "I don't want to achieve immortality through art. I want to achieve it by not dying.") I had to moderate my point by saying, when we are raised, it is *God* who does the work, not because of something intrinsic to our nature.

And then I have also been asked the practical questions: What exactly will be the nature of my resurrected body? Will my father recognize me in heaven? On the other hand, can I cremate my grandmother? What will my disabled child look like? From the sketch presented so far, the critical element in our resurrected *bodies* as the New Testament understands it is not our flesh and bones. It is *our concrete selves*. Generally, Eastern religious traditions, such as Buddhism and Hinduism, describe a state in which our individuality disappears. Buddha talked about the transition from one life to the next (remember, we keep migrating from one body to the next in Eastern thought) as a flame being passed from one candle to another. Alternatively, we become a drop of water in the ocean of Being. Instead, the Christian faith believes that God will raise us as concrete individuals, who altogether comprise God's people. Ultimately, because it is God's work, we can cremate or bury because our resurrection does not depend on flesh and bones. (Specifically, how else can we understand God's promise of a perfected, whole body in the resurrection for a victim of a violent dismemberment?) Our resurrected bodies will be us, but freed from the defects inherent in a fallen world.

We will recognize one another in heaven. Who and what we are on earth represents the concrete self that God created. The body-soul unity that now comprises us will dissolve at death, but our individuality—the "pattern of information" is another metaphor—will be instantly re-created at death into the resurrected body. The English writer Susan Howatch—who made her own headlines by funding a chair at Oxford in science and theology—describes this doctrine in her novel *The Wonder Worker*. She presents a dialogue on the bodily resurrection between a confused agnostic, Alice, and an Anglican priest, Nicholas Darrow, using the contemporary analogy of information. Alice's aunt has just been cremated.

"But if Aunt's now ashes, how can one talk of a resurrection of the body?"

"'Body' in that context is probably a code-word for the whole person. When we say 'anybody' or 'everybody' or 'somebody' we're not talking about flesh and blood—we're referring to the complex pattern of information which the medium of flesh and blood expresses."

I struggled to wrap my mind around this. "So you're saying that flesh and blood are more or less irrelevant?"

"No, not irrelevant. Our bodies have a big impact on our development as people—they constitute the pattern of information, and in fact we wouldn't be people without them. But once we're no longer confined by space and time the flesh and blood become superfluous and the pattern can be downloaded elsewhere. . . . Do you know anything about computers?"

"No."

"Okay, forget that, think of Michelangelo instead. In the Sistine Chapel he expressed a vision by creating, through the medium of paint, patterns of colour. The paint is of vital importance but in the end it's the pattern that matters and the pattern which can be reproduced in another medium such as a book or film."[82]

Indeed, in any medium, the Sistine Chapel depicts with stunning beauty the full sweep of God's first through final act in history. It also provides another illustration of eschatology. Scanning from the ceiling to altar, another vision meets the eye—Christ judging the world.

The Last Judgment

Michelangelo Buonarroti began painting the ceiling of the Sistine Chapel at the age of thirty-five. It was 1510 and it would be seven years until Martin Luther nailed his Ninety-five Theses to the Wittenberg Castle church door to initiate the Protestant Reformation. But from 1536 to 1541, as he labored on the fresco of *The Last Judgment,* Rome was feeling the impact of the Protestant revolt against its religious authority. In Michelangelo's enduring artistic image of Christ's judging the world, Christ pronounces the fate of all humankind with awesome finality. The 314 figures clearly divide into two groups. One is raised into the glories of heaven with the apostles and the patriarchs. The other, the damned, cower in abject despair. In light of the religious controversies of the day, significantly one man is barely saved by hanging onto the rosary, a symbol of medieval Catholic devotion to the Virgin Mary. In addition, as the Princeton theologian Daniel Migliore comments, "The martyrs of the faith who surround Christ seem to take satisfaction in the torment of the damned."[83] And there Michelangelo—surely one of the world's greatest artists and intellectuals—reveals a base flaw. His view of the final judgment—and often ours as well—conflates a sincere devotion to God's sovereignty with a touch of hate for our foes.

Jesus Christ is the antidote to these unhelpful notions. In him, we certainly meet our Judge. Yes, Christ will judge all people. Yes, he will root out evil. But this Judge is also our Savior. I gained a valuable insight from Karl Barth on the nature of Christ's judgment: the only God we know as Christians is the God who is *for us,* the God revealed in Jesus Christ. Or, as Migliore writes, "the very same Christ who was crucified and raised for us will also be our judge on the final day."[84] Jesus walked on the streets and taught God's grace. Jesus sat at table with his disciples, saying, "Take and eat. This is my body broken for you." This judge gave himself for us. Paul says it best in the final verses of Romans 8 as he lifts his rhetoric to truly heavenly heights:

> For I am convinced that neither death, nor life, nor angels, nor rulers, nor things present, nor things to come, nor powers, nor height, nor depth, nor anything else in all creation, will be able to separate us from the love of God in Christ Jesus our Lord. (Rom. 8:38–39)

Michelangelo's work also opened up the imposing question of heaven and hell, to which I now turn.

Heaven and Hell

A moment ago, I remarked that Michelangelo revealed a common human desire for our enemies' demise. Maybe that is not the whole story. Perhaps we can find another thread. When I first typed *hell* into my laptop, *heal* came out. Significant? Perhaps. I—like many of us—hope that God will heal Hitler, and Stalin, and the obnoxiously loud next-door neighbor, and the rabid atheist professor so that they all would turn to the Light. In a word, I hope for a life with no hell.

The Bible is much more interested in heaven than in hell. So we ought to start there. It is the direction creation has pointed from the beginning. In fact, with the consummation of creation in mind, Genesis 1–2 receives new light. The Lord calls the world "good," not only in its initial form, but because God will remain faithful to creation and lead it continually toward perfection. Put in a different way, we fully understand the goodness of the first act of creation in light of the final act of new creation.

In the prophets, Isaiah stands out, describing of the promise of the future and insights into creation. As Israel experienced increasing national trauma after its defeat and subsequent occupation by the hated and indomitable Babylonians in the sixth century B.C., several prophets looked with hope to a coming day—the day of the promised victory by God's Messiah. Several passages in the second part of Isaiah (chaps. 40–66) link eschatological hope with the creation at the beginning. For example, Isaiah promises a new day of hope for the exiled people in which the natural order will return, subduing chaos as in Genesis 1, and restoring creation in some form to Eden:

> For the LORD will comfort Zion;
>   he will comfort all her waste places,
> and will make her wilderness *like Eden,*
>   her desert like the garden of the LORD;
> joy and gladness will be found in her,
>   thanksgiving and the voice of song.
>   (Isa. 51:3, italics mine)

The final chapters of the Bible, Revelation 21 and 22, provide a vision of another city, the City of God. In it ceaseless praise of God continues. Beautiful music (jazz?) fills the heavenly city. And there is continual activity. We are not simply given rest in heaven, but work without the curse of futility. ("By the sweat of your face you shall eat bread until you return to the ground" Gen. 3:19a.) The final words offer two great promises: "Blessed are those who wash their robes, so that they will have the right to the tree of life and may enter the city by the gates" (Rev. 22:14). In this vision of cleansing and glory, we can take hold of the tree that Adam and Eve were forced to avoid after their disobedience (Gen. 3:24). As a final act of triumph, Jesus will return to right our turbulent world, where God's people face persecution:

> The one who testifies to these things says, "Surely I am coming soon."
> Amen. Come, Lord Jesus!
> The grace of the Lord Jesus be with all the saints. Amen.
> (Rev. 22:20–21)

In 1994 the author (and now speaker) Betty Eadie sold boatloads of her book *Embraced by the Light,* which describes her near-death experiences. Shortly after the book was published, I studied Eadie's revelations with a church adult education class. We were struck by the specific and comforting details she described about heaven. In many ways, we simply *wanted* to believe them. On the other hand, we know the difficulty of assessing the truth of these descriptions by Eadie or other similar authors like Dannion Brinkely (*Saved by the Light: The True Story of a Man Who Died Twice and the Profound Revelations He Received*) and Raymond A. Moody Jr. (*Life after Life: The Investigation of a Phenomenon—Survival of Bodily Death*). Broadly, they confirm some type of afterlife. Nevertheless, the interest in Eadie's book reveals that Americans crave to know precisely what happens "on the other side." Will I see my mother again? Will I understand why my son died of cancer at age nine? Will my dog be in heaven? The Bible offers a more profound answer, but does not satisfy every speculation. *The Bible concerns itself foremost with God's justice to right a world distorted by sin and secondly with God's salvation of a people.* We are left without exhaustive detail of what happens to each of us individually. God will create a fully just world where the people of God will—for the first time—live fully human lives, thereby glorifying their Creator.

And so we arrive at the unpleasant doctrine of hell. I would be glad to forget all about it. It is not only unpopular ("There you Christians go again with your judging!"), but personally repelling (remember, I want everyone to be healed). But unfortunately we hear it in Scripture and particularly on the lips of Jesus. It also makes sense of free will (what if some continue to resist God?) and God's sovereignty (can a good God allow the unrepentant to exist forever?). Some biblical scholars—notably the prominent English evangelical, John Stott—have taken a fresh look and determined that hell cannot be everlasting, conscious punishment. His work demonstrates the need to look again at this terrible doctrine. My hope is that we will be able to put aside any notions we have read in Dante's poetry or seen on *The Omen* and listen attentively to the Scripture.

First of all, what does *hell* mean? Beginning with the key words is often a good approach. *Sheol* and *Hades* are transliterations of Hebrew and Greek words respectively that simply mean the abode of the dead, not necessarily a place of punishment. In the New Testament, hell translates a Greek term, *geenna,* which was originally the name of a garbage dump in the Valley of Hinnom, in which children ritually were later killed and dedicated to the god Moloch and dumped as refuse. This pit burned day and night. At the time of Christ, it had became a symbol for a place of end-times punishment.

C. S. Lewis, exercising his skills as a literary critic, analyzes the key texts on hell in the Gospels. He demonstrates that there are three primary images: punishment (the "eternal punishment" of Matt. 25:46), destruction (Matt. 10:28's "fear him who can destroy both soul and body in hell"), and finally privation and banishment (the "outer darkness" where the slave who hid his talents in Matt. 25:30 is sent). Lewis comments, "It is not necessary to concentrate on the images of torture to the exclusion of those suggesting destruction and privation."[85] He continues by looking again at the conclusion of the parable of the sheep and goats (especially Matt. 25:34, 41).

[T]he damned go to a place never made for men at all. To enter heaven is to become more human than you ever succeeded in being in earth; to enter hell, is to be banished from humanity. What is cast (or casts itself) into hell is not a man: it is "remains."[86]

If there is existence in hell, it is a shadowy one. Lewis adds one final reflection on the biblical texts: Jesus emphasizes finality, not duration in these texts. "Consignment to the destroying fire is usually treated as the end of the story—not as the beginning of a new story."[87]

I must add one note to Lewis. There is also a tension in Scripture between final exclusion and an ultimate healing. First Timothy 2:4 affirms that God "desires everyone to be saved and to come to the knowledge of the truth." A note of universalism also finds its way in the stirring conclusion to 1 Corinthians 15: "[F]or all of us die in Adam, so all will be made alive in Christ." And a cryptic verse in 1 Peter describes Christ preaching to perished souls. Verse 19 says that after his death, he "went and made a proclamation to the spirits in prison, who in former times did not obey."

So in the end, will all be saved? Will "hell" finally end up in "heal"? Calvin notoriously saw two rooms into which we were born and elected by the sovereign God—either heaven or hell. The doors are locked, and the decision irrevocable. But what if we look specifically to the God we know in Jesus Christ? What if we begin with Christ as the elect Representative for all humanity? By his work, we begin in the embrace of God's love and therefore in the party room of election. The room is, however, not locked. It is of course our choice to move out into the outer darkness. Will God's ultimate plan for salvation triumph even over our bad decisions? Perhaps this question cannot be solved theoretically, but through prayer—that we are to pray for a redemption far beyond what we could imagine. Perhaps we are to pray for an embrace that includes our cynical coworker, the rapist who terrorized our streets, and even the most hated and cruel, like the emperor Nero and Adolf Hitler.

The Importance of Hope

What difference does it make that Christ guarantees a great future? God's new creation has a very personal focus as well. It is central to God's ability to change us. God does not just create at the beginning, but continues to bring forth life. The Creator does not simply fashion the cosmos, but offers us the opportunity to be "in Christ" as "a new creation" (2 Cor. 5:17). The Lord sees through what we are now to what we will become.

The new creation meets us on any Sunday, as we receive the Lord's Supper. In this meal, God's new creation, begun with Christ's resurrection on Easter and pointing toward fulfillment in the new creation, meets us in the here and now. Yes, I realize Communion happens as we sit behind a woman with too much perfume, while the man next to us sings "Amazing Grace" off key, and while our minds race to construct a shopping list for Sunday dinner. Still, in the midst of those human irritations and distractions, the Holy One meets us.

My invitation to the Lord's Supper begins with a reference to Luke 13:29's call to the eschatological party:

> Friends, this is joyful feast of the people of God!
> They will come from east and west
> And from north and south,
> And sit at table in the kingdom of God.

Too often our worship remains heavy and somber, especially in the Lord's Supper. But there we taste heaven and resurrection power. And so, on the final page of his outline of the Christian faith, Barth writes, "The Lord's Supper ought to be more firmly regarded from the Easter standpoint, than is generally the case. It is not primarily a mourning or funeral meal, but the anticipation of the marriage feast of the Lamb."[88]

The end of the world leads us toward *hope*. Hope is not Karl Marx's famous "opiate of the people," a device of social control to keep down social unrest. Hope, as Soskice comments, essentially leads to action: "Hope, like faith and love, is a state of readiness, and hope, like faith and love, is only displayed in action."[89] It leads scientists to experiment, mothers to work to sustain the families, fathers to keep changing diapers. Without hope, the future vanishes. And without a future, there is no action.

A few years ago, Stephen Covey, in his multimillion seller *The Seven Habits of Highly Effective People,* reminded Americans to "keep the end in mind." Covey's advice is good. We have to know where we are headed in order to get there. And that direction gives purpose and meaning to the journey. Keeping this end in mind— the purposes of God for the world—brings hope as it transforms everything we do. Why? Scripture describes an astounding ending to the drama to those who are ready. When the final curtain call comes, the very Scriptwriter will step onto the stage. Applauding us, the Author of our lives and all history will greet us with these words: "Well done." And then we are given a promising future: "I will put you in charge of many things; enter into the joy of your master." Those words give our lives meaning. That indeed is the end to keep in mind.

Notes

1. Shakespeare, *As You Like It,* 2.1, cited in Timothy Ferris, *Coming of Age in the Milky Way,* 217.

2. Margaret Geller, cited in John F. Haught, "Evolution, Tragedy, and Hope," in *Science and Theology: The New Consonance,* ed. Ted Peters, 229.

3. e. e. cummings, *100 Selected Poems,* 114.

4. George Lemaître, cited in Ferris, *Coming of Age,* 211.

5. Ibid., 208.

6. Fred Hoyle, *Facts and Dogmas in Cosmology and Elsewhere* (Cambridge: Cambridge University Press, 1982), 2f, cited in Christopher Southgate et al., *God, Humanity, and the Cosmos,* 36.

7. COBE home page: http://space.gsfc.nasa.gov/astro/cobe/cobe.

8. Robert Jastrow, *God and the Astronomers,* 125.

9. Augustine, *Confessions,* tr. R. S. Pine-Coffin, XI.14, 263–64.

10. Thomas C. Oden, *The Living God: Systematic Theology,* vol. 1, 63.

11. C. S. Lewis, *Reflections on the Psalms,* 137–38.

12. Blaise Pascal, *Pensées,* tr. A. J. Krailsheimer, rev. ed., no. 47, p. 13.

13. Wayne Muller, *Sabbath,* 40.

14. Stanley Grenz, *A Primer on Postmodernism,* 56. See also 40–44.

15. Thomas Aquinas, *Summa Theologiae* I, Q. 45, art. 6, cited in Oden, *Living God,* 48.

16. Catherine Mowry LaCugna, *God for Us,* 225.

17. Pascal, *Pensées,* nos. 781, 463, pp. 236–37, 151.

18. John Updike, *Roger's Version,* 32.

19. Dava Sobel, *Galileo's Daughter,* 11.

20. Margaret Wertheim, *Pythagoras' Trousers,* 7.

21. Charles E. Hummel, *The Galileo Connection,* 126.

22. Stephen Weinberg, in the *New York Review of Books,* October 21, 1999, cited in the *Christian Century,* January 26, 2000.

23. James Clerk Maxwell, cited in Hummel, *Galileo Connection,* 253.

24. Ian Barbour, *When Science Meets Religion,* chap. 1.

25. Philip Johnson, *Darwin on Trial,* 2d ed., 161.

26. Galileo, Letter to Nicolas-Claude Fabri de Peiresc, cited in Sobel, *Galileo's Daughter,* 314.

27. Copernicus, cited in Hummel, *Galileo Connection,* 39.

28. Charles Towne, in Ted Peters, ed., *Science and Theology,* 46.

29. Max Jammer, *Einstein and Religion,* 31.

30. Opening letter to George V. Coyne, quoted in Russell et al., eds., *Physics, Philosophy, and Theology,* M13.

31. Asa Gray, cited in Hummel, *Galileo Connection,* 232–33.

32. Dietrich Bonhoeffer, *Letter and Papers from Prison,* ed. Eberhard Bethge, 282.

33. Pascal, *Pensées,* no. 808, pp. 244–45.

34. Stephen Weinberg, *The First Three Minutes,* 149.

35. From the *Tao Te Ching,* cited in Huston Smith, *The World's Great Religions,* 279.

36. Bertrand Russell, quoted in James Bryant Conant, *Modern Science and Modern Man,* 139–40.

37. Charles Darwin, *Origin of Species by Means of Natural Selection, or the Preservation of Favoured Races in the Struggle for Life* (London: John Murray, 1859), 115, 131, 153, 155, cited in Southgate et al., *God, Humanity, and the Cosmos,* 140.

38. Keith Miller, *Finding Darwin's God,* 51.

39. Ibid., 292.

40. Richard Dawkins, "On Debating Religion," *The Nullfidian* (December 1994), cited in Miller, *Finding Darwin's God,* 254.

41. T. H. Huxley, cited in Ferris, *Coming of Age,* 245.

42. Henry Drummond, *The Ascent of Man,* 45–46, cited in Claude Welch, *Protestant Thought in the Nineteenth Century,* 2:207–8.

43. Charles Hodge, *Systematic Theology* 1:168–70, cited in Welch, *Protestant Thought,* 2:199.

44. Richard Dawkins, *The Blind Watchmaker,* xi.

45. Stephen Jay Gould, "Evolution's Erratic Pace," *Natural History,* May 1977, 12.

46. Charles Darwin, letter, November 29, 1859, cited in David L. Hull, *Darwin and His Critics,* 9.

47. "Evolution and the Bible," in "Selected Theological Statements of the Presbyterian Church (U.S.A.)." For the full text, see: http://www.pcusa.org/taw/evolutionstatement.htm.

48. Dawkins, *The Blind Watchmaker,* 2d ed., x; italics mine.

49. John Calvin, *Genesis,* 86.

50. Miller, *Finding Darwin's God,* 257.

51. John Polkinghorne and Michael Welker, eds., *The End of the World and the Ends of God,* 80.

52. Barbour, *When Science Meets Religion,* 57–58 (I have shortened the quotation somewhat). The Stephen Hawking citation is from his *A Brief History of Time,* 121.

53. Barbour, *When Science Meets Religion,* 58.

54. Stephen Meyer, "Qualified Agreement: Modern Science and the Return of the 'God Hypothesis,'" in Richard F. Carlson, *Science and Christianity: Four Views,* 149. Meyer cites Barrow and Tipler, *The Anthropic Cosmological Principle* (Oxford: Oxford University Press, 1986), 295–356, 384–444, 510–56; and Penrose, *The Emperor's New Mind* (New York: Oxford, 1983), 188.

55. Freeman Dyson, *Disturbing the Universe* (New York: Harper & Row, 1979), 256.

56. J. Boslough, *Stephen Hawking's Universe* (New York: William Morrow, 1985), 121.

57. Lynn White, "The Historical Roots of our Ecologic Crisis," 1203–7.

58. Niles Eldridge, cited in Edward J. Larson and Larry Witham, "Scientists and Religion in America," *Scientific American,* September 1999, 92.

59. Vincent van Gogh, cited in Don Postema, *Space for God,* 68.

60. Alfred North Whitehead, *Religion in the Making,* 77.

61. Richard Dawkins, *River out of Eden,* 132–33, cited in Polkinghorne, *Belief in God in an Age of Science,* 12.

62. John Polkinghorne, *Science and Theology: An Introduction,* 63–64.

63. Pierre-Simon de Laplace, cited in Ferris, *Coming of Age,* 291.

64. Francis Crick, *The Astonishing Hypothesis,* 3.

65. Ted Peters, *Playing God?* 176.

66. Werner Heisenberg, *Physics and Philosophy,* e.g., 180f.

67. Robert Russell, "Does the 'God Who Acts' Really Act in Nature?" In Peters, ed., *Science and Theology,* 89.

68. Polkinghorne, *Faith of a Physicist,* 169.

69. Oden, *The Living God,* 272–73.

70. John Stott, *Romans,* 246–48.

71. Ibid., 248.

72. From an unpublished early draft of the new Presbyterian catechism; used by permission of George Hunsinger.

73. Scripture taken from Eugene H. Peterson, *The Message: The New Testament in Contemporary Language* (Colorado Springs, Colo.: NavPress, 1996). Copyright © by Eugene H. Peterson, 1993, 1994, 1995, 1996. Used by permission of NavPress Publishing Group.

74. Lewis, *The Problem of Pain,* 10.

75. Ernest Becker, *The Denial of Death,* ix.

76. Polkinghorne, *Faith of a Physicist,* 162.

77. William Stoeger, cited in Polkinghorne and Welker, *End of the World,* 19–28.

78. Polkinghorne, *Faith of a Physicist,* 162.

79. Cicero, *Orations,* cited in F. F. Bruce, *Philippians,* 79.

80. C. S. Lewis, *The World's Last Night, and Other Essays,* 107f.

81. Ibid., 113.

82. Susan Howatch, *The Wonder Worker,* 44.

83. Daniel Migliore, *Faith Seeking Understanding,* 244.

84. Ibid., 245.

85. Lewis, *Problem of Pain,* 124–25.

86. Ibid., 125.

87. Ibid., 127.

88. Karl Barth, *Dogmatics in Outline,* 155.

89. Polkinghorne and Welker, *End of the World,* 86.

Works Cited

Augustine. *Confessions.* Translated by R. S. Pine-Coffin. Harmondsworth, Middlesex: Penguin, 1961.

Barbour, Ian. *When Science Meets Religion.* New York: HarperSanFrancisco, 2000.

Barth, Karl. *Dogmatics in Outline.* Translated by G. T. Thomson. New York: Harper & Row, 1959.

Becker, Ernest. *The Denial of Death.* New York: Free Press, 1973.

Bonhoeffer, Dietrich. *Letters and Papers from Prison.* Edited by Eberhard Bethge. Translated by Reginald Fuller, Frank Clark, John Bouden, et al. New York: Collier, 1972.

Bruce, F. F. *Philippians.* New International Biblical Commentary. Peabody, Mass.: Hendrickson, 1989.

Butin, Philip W. *The Trinity.* Louisville, Ky.: Geneva, 2000.

Calvin, John. *Genesis.* Translated by John King. Carlisle, Pa.: Banner of Truth Trust, 1965.

———. *Institutes of the Christian Religion.* Vol. 20. *The Library of Christian Classics.* Edited by John T. McNeil. Translated by Ford Lewis Battles. 2 vols. Philadelphia: Westminster, 1960 (1559).

Cameron, Kathryn J. *Why Have You Forsaken Me?* Louisville, Ky.: Geneva, forthcoming.

Carlson, Richard F. *Science and Christianity: Four Views.* Downers Grove, Ill.: InterVarsity, 2000.

Conant, James Bryant. *Modern Science and Modern Man.* New York: Doubleday, 1953.

Crick, Francis. *The Astonishing Hypothesis: The Scientific Search for the Soul.* New York: Scribner, 1994.

cummings, e. e. *100 selected poems.* New York: Grove, 1926.

Dawkins, Richard. *The Blind Watchmaker: Why the Evidence of Evolution Reveals a Universe without a Design.* New York: Norton, 1987. 2d ed., with a new Introduction, 1996.

————. *River out of Eden: A Darwinian View of Life.* New York: Harper-Collins, 1995.

Ferris, Timothy. *Coming of Age in the Milky Way.* Garden City, N.Y.: Doubleday, 1989.

Grenz, Stanley. *A Primer on Postmodernism.* Grand Rapids: Eerdmans, 1996.

Hawking, Stephen. *A Brief History of Time.* New York: Bantam, 1988.

Heisenberg, Werner. *Physics and Philosophy: The Revolution in Modern Science.* New York: Harper & Row, 1958.

Howatch, Susan. *The Wonder Worker.* New York: Alfred A. Knopf, 1997.

Hull, David L. *Darwin and His Critics: The Reception of Darwin's Theory of Evolution by the Scientific Community.* Cambridge, Mass.: Harvard University Press, 1973.

Hummel, Charles E. *The Galileo Connection: Resolving Conflicts between Science and the Bible.* Downers Grove, Ill.: InterVarsity, 1986.

Jammer, Max. *Einstein and Religion: Physics and Theology.* Princeton, N.J.: Princeton University Press, 1999.

Jastrow, Robert. *God and the Astronomers.* New York: Basic Books, 1980.

Johnson, Philip. *Darwin on Trial.* 2d ed. Downers Grove, Ill.: InterVarsity, 1993.

LaCugna, Catherine Mowry. *God for Us: The Trinity and Christian Life.* San Francisco: Harper & Row, 1991.

Larson, Edward J., and Larry Witham. "Scientists and Religion in America." *Scientific American,* vol. 281, no. 3: 88–93.

Lewis, C. S. (Clive Staples). *The Problem of Pain.* New York: Macmillan, 1962.

————. *Reflections on the Psalms.* New York: Harcourt Brace Jovanovich, 1958.

————. *The World's Last Night and Other Essays.* New York: Harcourt Brace Jovanovich, 1959.

Migliore, Daniel. *Faith Seeking Understanding.* Grand Rapids: Eerdmans, 1991.

Miller, Kenneth. *Finding Darwin's God.* New York: HarperTrade Cliff Street Books, 1999.

Muller, Wayne. *Sabbath: Finding Rest, Renewal, and Delight in Our Busy Lives.* New York: Bantam, 1999.

Oden, Thomas C. *The Living God, Systematic Theology: Volume One.* New York: HarperCollins, 1987.

Pascal, Blaise. *Pensées*. Translated by A. J. Krailsheimer. Revised edition. London: Penguin, 1995.

Peacocke, Charlie. *The Secret of Time*. Sparrow SPD 1217 (compact disc).

Peters, Ted. *Playing God? Genetic Determinism and Human Freedom*. New York: Routledge, 1996.

Peters, Ted, ed. *Science and Theology: The New Consonance*. Boulder: Westview, 1998.

Polkinghorne, John. *The Faith of a Physicist: Reflections of a Bottoms-Up Thinker*. Minneapolis: Fortress, 1994.

Polkinghorne, John, and Michael Welker, eds. *The End of the World and the Ends of God: Science and Theology on Eschatology*. Harrisburg, Pa.: Trinity, 2000.

Postema, Don. *Space for God: The Study and Practice and Spirituality*. Grand Rapids: Bible Way, 1983.

Russell, Robert John; William R. Stoeger, S. J.; George V. Coyne, S. J., editors. *Physics, Philosophy, and Theology: A Common Quest for Understanding*. Notre Dame: University of Notre Dame Press, 1988.

Selected Theological Statements of the Presbyterian Church (U.S.A.) General Assemblies (1956–1998). Louisville, Ky.: Presbyterian Church (U.S.A.), 1998.

Smith, Houston. *The World's Religions: Our Great Wisdom Traditions*. New York, HarperCollins, 1991.

Sobel, Dava. *Galileo's Daughter: A Historical Memoir of Science, Faith, and Love*. New York: Penguin Putnam, 2000.

Southgate, Christopher et al. *God, Humanity, and the Cosmos: A Textbook in Science and Religion*. Harrisburg, Pa.: Trinity, 1999.

Stott, John. *Romans: God's Good News for the World*. Downers Grove, Ill.: InterVarsity, 1994.

Updike, John. *Roger's Version*. New York: Chivers North America, 1988.

Van Dyk, Leanne. *Believing in Jesus Christ*. Louisville, Ky.: Geneva, forthcoming.

Weinberg, Stephen. *The First Three Minutes*. New York: Basic Books, 1977.

Welch, Claude. *Protestant Thought in the Nineteenth Century*. 2 volumes. Yale: Yale University Press, 1972, 1985.

Wertheim, Margaret. *Pythagoras' Trousers: God, Physics, and the Gender Wars*. New York: Times, 1995.

White, Lynn. "The Historical Roots of Our Ecologic Crisis." *Science* 155 (March 1967): 1203–7.

Whitehead, Alfred North. *Religion in the Making*. New York: Macmillan, 1926.